Billie's

A true story about adoption

Billie's Kid

A true story about adoption

Steve Tucker

First published 2015

ISBN 978-0-9934283-0-2

Printed and bound in the United Kingdom by SRP Ltd, Exeter.

Website: www.billieskid.com

FOREWORD

Adoption doesn't mean very much to most people. At best, we look upon those people who choose to adopt, and either we think that it is nice that they can have a child because they clearly couldn't have had one naturally, or we are grateful that some people seem keen to foster and adopt kids from troubled backgrounds.

In many ways, adoption is a tragedy. The need to adopt and the availability of the child for adoption are both founded in a tragedy of circumstance. I can't think of an example where someone would voluntarily create life in order to give it away to another; it is simply not the nature of things. Therefore, it follows that adopted children are the product of a life gone wrong, poor decision making, societal norms, bad judgment or poor timing. In essence, we adoptees are the by-products of non-conformism.

Steve Tucker is a child of the 60s. That, to most of us nowadays, is a long time ago – perhaps even an irrelevance in today's hectic world, something we only relate to in terms of rock 'n' roll, The Beatles, the Cuban missile crisis, to name but a few. However, in the world of adoption, it was the start of a new process that took over from the naming of illegitimate children as younger siblings, cousins or servants – as had been the norm. This was a time, barely thirty years on, from when, in 1928, women first got the right to vote. You may think thirty years is a long time, but I still remember, in 1987, my mother having a conversation with the bank manager, where she was told he could only speak to the "man" of the house. My point is that thirty years is nothing in terms of social change. It is simply the time it takes for a baby to become a grown man; it is a generation.

I say all of this simply to put the idea of adoption into some sort of context. It is only since 1926 that we have had any legislation from parliament that puts adoption on a legal footing. The first adoptees are now, like our First World War veterans, coming to the end of an era. There is no question that adoption was a superb solution to a social problem – a win-win in modern parlance. Those in need were provided for by those who were also in need. However, along the way, we have forgotten some fairly deep-rooted and fundamental aspects of this service. No matter how good their lives have been, adoptees will at some stage in their lives reflect on the fact that they are a result of rejection. They have all been rejected, either consciously or through tragic circumstances. Both of these options are a source of hurt to the adopted child and play a role in shaping how the child sees the world. Adoptees will seek their biological parents in order to answer questions they have about either who they are and where they come from, or why they were given up for adoption. Each child, whether consciously or unconsciously, must reconcile this in some manner in order to find some acceptance of his or her circumstances.

Billie's Kid is such a journey. Like Steve, I was adopted in the 60s, but my reconciliation was very different in that I had no desire to search for my biological parents.

Steve has a story telling gift. By his own admission, he is not a writer and has struggled with the writing of this book. However, something inside him clearly needed to write about his experiences. As a fellow adoptee, I don't mind admitting to being deeply affected by his book. I learned a new perspective and a new level of sympathy for my biological mother that I had not considered before. It helped me to explain my attitudes towards society, dishonesty and women's rights and went a long way to explaining some aspects of who I am. If, like me, the reader is adopted, then it will be difficult not to be affected by the story and many of the issues raised in it.

As adoptees, we are silent and willing participants in our own care. We are at one level a survivor and at another a gift, a special person, a giver of hope, love and joy to our adoptive parents. We are a living paradox of our circumstances. The adopted child has to be extraordinary because of these relationships.

You will find a bit of everything in this book depending on who you are and what your attitude is towards the subject matter. As such, I have no hesitation in recommending it to you.

Andrew Wilson

ACKNOWLEDGEMENTS

Grateful acknowledgement is made to:

Barbara Wilson, at Southmoor Editing, for her on-going editorial support and belief in my work. (www.southmoor-editing.com)

My close friend Mark Goldsborough for being my best friend for over forty years. Thank you for your honesty, encouragement and belief in my writing.

Andrew Wilson for giving me confidence that my story was worth telling and for writing the foreword to this book.

Penny Mark Billson, my blood mother's best friend of thirty years, for her guidance and friendship throughout my difficult journey and during the writing of this book.

Maria Douglas for her friendship with my blood mother, her contribution for this book and her explanations of my unfamiliar and mysterious experiences.

The Brighton crew for their love and friendship with my blood mother. You know who you are.

Rose Boyce for her trust in me, for our new family friendship right from the start (something that was really important to me) and for providing written input for this book.

Duncan Jones, from Duncan Jones Graphic Design, for all the Billie's Kid design and artwork. I also thank you for being one of Billie's best friends. (www.djdesign.co.uk)

My wife and family for their continued support whilst I explored an unknown and very scary world, one where things could easily have got very complicated and have gone terribly wrong – and sometimes did during my search. I thank you and also apologise.

And finally to my parents for choosing me, keeping me safe, guiding me through life's ups-and-downs, looking after me and always being there for me. I will always love you and thank you for everything. RIP, Dad. I wouldn't be here if it wasn't for you. Also to my sister, who will hopefully forgive me and one day understand me for just being me.

Introduction

I spent the night at hospital feeling very nervous and excited; my wife and I were having our first child. This was a whole new experience for me. All the obvious things that new fathers think about were going through my mind. Will it be okay? Will it be healthy? Will my wife's body ever get back to normal? Will I be able to cope once the baby arrives? Will I be a good dad? But even more important for me was that I was waiting to see – for the very first time in my life – a member of my blood family. I had been adopted in 1961 and had never seen, met, talked to or loved a blood relative before.

Our baby boy was born and, on that momentous day, I saw someone who looked like me and carried my genes. I had spent all of my life wondering who I was, where I had come from and asking myself whether anybody out there looked like me. Even on that first day, as I was holding him in my arms, I could see my eyes staring back at me. His palm creases were the same as mine; his nose was the same shape as mine; he even had the same distinctive little mark on his left cheek.

I examined his feet in amazement – the markings, the lines. He definitely came from the same box of chocolates as me, bought in the same department store and from the same town. I was totally besotted by him. His little ears were the same shape as mine; his skin tone, hair colour and facial shape the same – a little version of me, at last.

Every parent wants to tell the world about the birth of their first child but, for me, it was slightly different: apart from wanting to tell my parents and friends, I felt the need to tell my birth mother and father that they had a grandson.

This was the very first time that I had felt the need to trace my roots or find my blood parents. Being present at the birth of your first child is special for any father, but this was extra special for me. My adoptive parents didn't look like me. I have an adopted sister who looks nothing like me. I often wondered if people could tell we were different from normal families. I had spent most of my life searching for faces in crowds, wondering if they were related to me, watching and waiting for a wave or a smile and a nod of acknowledgement.

The idea of tracing my blood parents was overwhelming at this time. Was it just a strong, natural yearning, which would pass? My parents were still alive, for god's sake, and I really didn't want to hurt them in any way at all. They had offered me love and had given me a wonderful life – and still do. I had heard that most adoptees wait until their parents are dead before searching, not wanting to hurt them.

Perhaps I felt that I had enough on my plate with a newborn baby to look after and get to know. Was I ready to have my life, heart and soul thrown into a selfish search into my unknown past? I decided to wait and reflect on my new yearnings. I actually felt guilty and angry with myself. Why did I suddenly want more? My parents had been brilliant; I'd had a superb upbringing. I had a loving wife and a successful career as a jazz musician. And I'd just become a dad.

A couple of years later, we had our second child. This was another great experience but slightly different this time as my second son didn't have all the distinctive markings that I have. Don't get me wrong; he was definitely mine. He looked like me and his brother and his mum, but the colour of his hair was very different to ours. People used to ask me whether he'd got his hair colour from my mum. Of course, I didn't know.

It was a few years later that my curiosity about searching for my blood parents was reawakened. This time the catalyst was not a birth but a death: the sad passing away of my wife's mother. Her funeral was held in a small picturesque village in Devon, England. We had a full family gathering – well, all my wife's family were there. I noticed how similar many of them looked.

Seeing so many people with the same characteristics in one place had a major effect on me.

My wife's brothers are monozygotic twins (identical). Most people can't tell them apart – even I have a problem distinguishing which one is which sometimes. They share a special connection beyond that which ordinary siblings have. It's almost as if they have extraordinary supernatural qualities. Each of them is able to feel a physical sensation that is actually being experience by the other. For example, when one of them had a hip operation, the other – who lives hundreds of miles away – was able to feel the pain and discomfort both during and after his brother's operation.

They perform similar actions when they are apart, such as buying the same item in shops: a new jumper, same day, same size, same colour, same chain store. They often find themselves phoning each other at the exact same time only to get the engaged tone. They sometimes appear to know each other's thoughts by speaking simultaneously or finishing each other's sentences.

When I first met them, the one thing that really stood out was that they both had a very special relationship. My wife tells lots of stories of their teenage years. For a bit of fun, they would swap classes in school to confuse the teachers. They would share girlfriends; one would do the chatting up, and the other one would go on the date. When they were in their twenties, they had the same make and colour of car and dressed very much the same. They were – and still are – very competitive: if one buys a boat, the other has to buy a bigger one. There are many articles describing the special relationship of twins, but to see it close at hand is fascinating and a little bit scary.

All the nephews and nieces at the funeral looked very similar: eyes, build, hair colour – all the obvious things that most people see in their families everyday, and possibly take for granted. I stood alone that day, sad, lonely and confused, wondering if I looked like anyone. Do I have a brother or a sister out there with similar looks to me? Is my blood mother and father out there somewhere? Do I look like them? Do my children look like them? I am assured that my children do look like me. I love it when people tell me how much my boys look like me.

The boys were not at the funeral that day as they were too young. I stood and observed the similarities in my wife's family with fascination, curiosity and bags of jealousy. When I got home, I looked deep into my children's eyes, gave them a huge hug and thought to myself, I want to learn more about who I really am, where I came from and, more importantly, whether I look like anyone else.

Chapter 1

Throughout my life, I have always felt a bit out of place – as if I don't quite fit – and on the day of the funeral I decided I needed to have my questions answered. That day, I knew the time had come for me to look into who I really was and where I had come from.

I knew I was in a very safe and secure place in my mind. I had a lovely home of my own, with a beautiful wife and two wonderful children. My parents were still alive and in regular contact. They loved me, so why was I still yearning for answers and wanting more? I suppose, this is something only an adoptee can answer. I started to think of the whole adoption concept in great detail. Why would my birth mother want to give me up? Had I done something wrong? And why did my parents adopt me?

My parents couldn't have children, and it saddened me greatly to realise, for the first time, what they'd had to go through. The psychological strain on the relationship must have been very hard: my mother's pain and grief of never being able to experience pregnancy, never knowing the feeling of a life growing inside her, never seeing her baby on a sonogram monitor and, of course, never experiencing the actual birth process and holding her baby seconds after it is born. I'd never thought of my parents going through that amount of turmoil.

Some people consider the birth process as the essence of being a real woman – or a real mother – and feel the need to talk about it constantly and share their views with others. How did you have your children? What birth plan did you use? How long were you in labour? Did the baby take to your breast straight away? These are conversations I overhear in supermarket aisles all the time – admittedly around the baby sections. And let's not forget the father's part: being at the birth, helping with the birth, holding the baby moments after it is born, cutting the umbilical cord – all seemingly part of the bonding process with the child. Are all these things so important in being a good parent? Does it bring you closer together? A lot of women can give birth; not all women can be good mothers.

My father was a doctor. He would have had all the tests. He would have had access to all the miracle cures or treatments available at the time. He could have pulled a few strings; after all, he knew some of the top gynaecological consultants in London's Harley Street. And still they couldn't conceive a baby of their own. Having tried to conceive for many years and having taken many fertility tests, my parents eventually decided to adopt.

Many adoptees think that the love their adoptive parents have for them is not the same as it would have been if their adoptive parents had had their own biological child. As a result, they go through life thinking they were their parents' second choice. I suppose they were; I suppose I was.

When I started my research into adoption, I found very early on that the 1960s were extremely difficult and heart-breaking times for single mums living in the UK. At that time there were so many babies available for adoption due to the free-love/swinging era and the fact that contraception was not readily available. Unmarried mothers had little choice but to give their babies up for adoption. Half a million women went through this experience. They had not harmed their child in any way, yet they lost them to adoption. At that time it was not socially acceptable to be a single mum and have an illegitimate child, and, unlike today, the government did not provide financial support to unmarried mothers. Having a child out of wedlock was not a thing to consider. There was no abortion option; it was illegal at the time. You were completely on your own.

Before information was readily available on computers, tracing your family was an extremely hard and long-winded process. To start the process, you needed your original name and, armed with this, you could start the long trawl, looking through thousands of surnames in telephone directories, in old church records and in libraries, where they held microfiche records of births, marriages and deaths. This was in addition to contacting elderly relatives for pictures and snippets of information.

If you were adopted before 12 November 1975, you are currently required by law to receive counselling and an assessment before being allowed access to any vital information. If you were adopted after that date, you are not legally required to seek any counselling – but it is strongly advised, believe me.

I was adopted before 1975 and had to contact my local government authority adoption office before going any further. I couldn't do anything without their consent. I wrote to them explaining my situation. A few days later I received a telephone call from the office, offering me a date and time for an initial interview. This was to be a home visit by the area adoption manager – in my case, a lady called Sue.

She arrived on a Monday morning, bang on time, briefcase in hand. I opened the door with anticipation, introduced myself and invited her in. I took her coat and made her a cup of coffee. She seemed to know me. "You're a jazz musician, aren't you?" she asked. I told her that I was. "I've seen your band play a few times. You're really good," she said. When you play on stage and the lights are in your eyes, it's difficult to see faces in the audience. I didn't recognise her at all. I suppose my being a musician was a bit obvious as my lounge does look a bit like a music shop or recording studio.

She sat down and I tried to make her feel welcome. She was dressed in a short, black, low-cut dress, with a chunky, multi-coloured necklace and matching earrings. Her fingernails were long and over painted; I could see the layers of nail lacquer poured on top of the previous day's artistic effort. She wore black fishnet stockings and very high, pointed shoes. Her perfume was strong, cheap and potent, with a slight musky undertone. My

7

lounge now smelt like a charity shop. She must have sprayed herself all over in the car just before knocking on the door. Her face was heavy with foundation; her lipstick was bright red. Discreetly, I looked out the window at the world outside. I pondered whether any of my neighbours had seen her arrive and were wondering what I was up to.

She was an interesting looking woman – a bit flamboyant – but she certainly knew all about the ins and outs of the adoption process. Her job was seeking new parents to adopt and helping people like me find their long-lost families. She asked me many questions. Why did I want to search? What was I trying to gain by it? Why had I left it so long?

She asked about my adoption history – of course, I knew very little. She had lots of questions: had I had a confusing childhood knowing I was adopted, what were my parents like, what did they think of my sudden urge to find out more about my birth? She told me a story about one of her female clients, who had desperately wanted to meet up with her blood relatives. However, when contact had been made, they hadn't wanted anything to do with her. They had moved on, had a new family and didn't want to know anything about her. That's how they wanted it left. I think she was trying to tell me that I shouldn't get my hopes up.

She described to me the hurt and traumatic stress I could potentially cause by starting my search. It wasn't just about me; there would be others involved – my search could hurt other family members. I was naïve. Back then I didn't really know what she was talking about. I explained that I'd never really thought of that – well, apart from my parents who were still alive. They may get hurt, but they were wise and strong and could cope – or so I thought.

Sue told me that it was likely that I could go through all the searching and then have to deal with a possible rejection from my own blood mother. Apparently, this often happens. Many adoptees find their blood parents only to discover them to be cold and in denial. They are only marginally interested in meeting them, and it doesn't go any further. She asked me if I could handle that. I said I could but admitted it would be very hard.

A lot of unmarried ladies who had a child in the 1960s simply wanted to forget. They were ashamed of what they had done – what they had gone through – and just wanted to move on, to remarry and start a new family. It was their deepest, darkest secret. Some of them didn't even tell their new husbands or children.

I said I could cope, but this conversation with Sue was starting to prepare me for the ultimate rejection: being rejected by my blood mother for the second time. We adoptees live in fear of the idea of rejection, as we understand it to represent the situation where, for our entire lives, we have not been wanted by our parents. "So, am I to prepare myself for my blood parents not caring about me, or even thinking about me, or loving me?" I asked. "Yes," she replied.

When searching for relatives or family members – or even when trying to map out a family tree, which is very common and popular these days – you may be stepping on territory that is best left alone. Some people may ask why we want to know so much about our past when the future is more important and within our control. For me, my past has always been just as important as my future.

Some people may wonder whether we are looking for links to royalty, long-lost Viking warriors or perhaps a distant Anglo-Saxon cousin. That all sounds very romantic but, on the other hand, we could discover that our family members were all murderers, pillagers and imprisoned thieves.

People around me talk so openly about previous generations of their families having been successful pioneers in business or captains in the navy. They show me old, torn, dusty photographs of great grandfathers and tell me stories of how their grandmothers gave birth in a shed and the following day were out ploughing the fields. It hurts when I hear friends talking like this. It brings home to me the fact that I have no knowledge of my past – no photographs, no stories, no history. Obviously, my adoptive parents had grandparents, so I did hear stories of relatives working in the fields, and I saw the photographs to back it all up. But they were not my real relatives – it just wasn't the same.

I am constantly reminded of not having a past. The classic question that is asked many times by health professionals is whether a certain disease runs in the family. They are always asking about any family history of this illness or that problem. I just have to quietly and politely say, "Sorry, I don't know, I was adopted." I've had to repeat this so many times. It's probably on my private medical records to this day: "This person has no medical history. He was adopted." When I was a child at primary school, I once saw my school medical records. In big, bold, blood-red letters, at the top of every page, it read: "THIS CHILD IS ADOPTED!"

As an inquisitive adopted child, my past was very important to me. I needed to know more; I didn't know anything at all. In order to proceed, Sue needed my birth certificate. She also told me to get prepared for the fact that my name may have been changed. I may be someone else on my original paperwork. I hadn't thought of that either.

Sue was convinced that I was serious about my search: no ulterior motives of gold digging, looking for family money or purposely trying to hurt anyone. But she did want to know a lot more about me before she was going any further. She insisted on knowing more about my life story and said we would have to have another meeting to discuss this. She said most, if not all, adoptees have at some stage gone off the rails a bit or have had a very difficult time. She asked if I had experienced anything like that. I told her I had, and we decided to talk about it at our next meeting.

She stood up to go and asked if she could buy one of my CDs as she really liked my band. I gave her one. I couldn't charge her; I think I was trying to impress her. I was desperately hoping that she would take me into her portfolio of long-lost people in search of their long-lost past.

Sue's visit certainly motivated me, but it worried me at the same time. I started researching the Internet for websites designed to give people like me information. It very quickly became clear that I was not the only one who was inquisitive about the word adoption or trying to find out more about my past. There are many sites available. With a bit of basic research, you can easily find the reputable ones and understand how they work. At this time, I had not yet learned my original birth name, so I was restricted in what I could search for.

I started by joining Genes Reunited; however, in order to search, it is necessary to know your blood parents' names. I didn't have my birth certificate. I'd never needed it. I'd never had a full ten-year passport – you need your birth certificate to apply for that. I had travelled a bit but mostly as a child on my parents' passports. And the few times I had ventured abroad, touring with bands, a year's temporary passport from the post office had been sufficient. But now I needed the certificate. Because I had moved around so much in my youth, my parents had always kept my personal documents. I realised that I now needed to involve my adoptive parents. Their relationship was strong, so I decided to let them know that I was going to be searching for my blood parents. I needed to ask them if they had my birth certificate at home.

Telling them of my intention to seek out my blood parents was a complete shock to them. Why would you want to do that? What are you looking for? Weren't we good enough for you? Why do you want more? I think adopted people always want more – more of everything – I know I do.

Most people wait until their parents have passed away before starting their search – out of respect, I suppose, and not wanting to hurt them. I was nearly fifty when I started searching in a serious way. I thought my parents were strong enough to accept my quest, and Mum was still one of my best friends. Could she and Dad cope with my new project?

I think my questions hurt my mother especially. I am sure she felt enormous pain in my desire to look further afield for new family members. I could hear the emotion in her voice when I told her on the phone. She is strong, experienced and wise, and she always wants the best for me, but I could hear the slight anger in her speech as she reacted to my explanation of why I needed to search for my blood mother. I am sure if the roles had been reversed, and I had an adopted son, I would feel exactly the same. I made too many assumptions that she would understand and be interested. I don't think I will ever know how much it hurt her. I hope that, one day, she will read my story and understand why I needed to know more about my life. But I suppose, if I'm honest, I don't think she will enjoy reading my book or gain any comfort in it at all. I am also worried about how she will react when she discovers it has been published. After she reads it, I think her comments are going to hurt. Sorry, Mum.

I think my mum had programmed herself, believing that she would never again have to think about my adoption – it was fifty years ago, for god's sake. It was like asking her to reboot her computer and search the archives in her trash box.

I asked Mum whether she had a copy of my adoption birth certificate, as I needed to send it with my request to the courts to release my original birth certificate and files. I mentioned to her that I would find out my original name at some stage. Mum then replied, "I think I might know that." Oops, my heart dropped. Why hadn't she told me that before? I suppose quite simply because I had never asked – well, never so directly anyway. I felt no anger or betrayal by the fact that she had possibly known and had not told me before. I was asking her now, though.

There was a pause in our conversation. Mum said she would phone me back as she wanted to check her paperwork and personal files. She reminded me this had taken place a very, very long time ago. Knowing her, she was probably going to check with Dad whether it was a good idea to give me the information.

A couple of hours later, Mum called back to tell me she had found my adoption birth certificate. She mentioned that she had also found some of her notes, handwritten at the time of my adoption. She told me she hadn't looked at the notes since the adoption and that she had forgotten she had written them. Then she told me what was written on them. "Your name was Clive Anthony Parsons. That was your birth name," she said. Then, straight away, she said firmly, "But your name is Stephen; don't ever forget that."

This was a huge emotionally confusing piece of information she had just given to me. I had always been known as Steve, or Stephen, to my mum and to my friends, and now I was staring into the mirror thinking … Clive? My first reaction was: "But I don't look like a Clive." Then I was angry; I didn't like the name Clive. I cried while on the phone to Mum. I tried to cover it up and pull myself together by chain-smoking whilst on the phone. It was too early in the day for a glass of scotch for Dutch courage. We ended the phone call, and she said she would send me the certificate by first-class post.

Bloody Clive! I mean no disrespect to anyone called Clive reading this, but I suddenly hated the name; it had images of a pen-pushing, sad, lonely office worker, who had no friends, lived by himself and went to the cinema once a week for fun, or a British colonial military serviceman in a pith helmet with a pencil-thin moustache, gold monocle, smoking a pipe and holding a pair of binoculars, dressed in some lavish khaki number.

I searched the Internet but struggled to find any distinguished musicians, pop stars, artists or film stars with the name Clive. To me, it wasn't an inspiring, creative name, at all. If you were called Clive and went into the music business, you would probably change it. I felt let down by my blood parents for calling me Clive – silly, I know, but I did. According to the Urban Dictionary of Names, Clive means the god of biceps. Every time he makes an entrance, universes collide, the sun explodes and black holes swallow themselves. Well that pretty much summed up how I felt. What a stupid name!

I remembered that this was one of the things Sue had warned me about. She'd told me it could take the wind out of my sails. It certainly did. I felt totally displaced for days.

However, at last, I had my original surname: Parsons. Mum also gave me the location of my adoption. I spent days searching the Internet. Parsons was a reasonably common name. In my imagination, telephone directory entries were starting to look like possible brothers, sisters and cousins. Was I now looking at my blood mother's address and telephone number? My curious and over-imaginative mind played tricks on me for days.

I sent the birth certificate off to Sue, along with details of my newly discovered name and adoption location, hoping it might help her with my search.

I put the surname into Facebook – again, hundreds of people called Parsons, and they had pictures of themselves! I stared at and stalked hundreds of them. Do I look like any of these people?

I started to join various websites. They all required a name and date of birth or death. I knew from my mum that my birth mother had had me later in life, rather than as a teenager. She told me roughly the age she might have been. I took a guess at all the options. Was she still alive? Had she passed away? Or – the very difficult research option – had she remarried and changed her surname or even moved abroad?

Parsons the butcher.
Parsons the baker.
Parsons the candlestick maker.
Which one am I looking for?

Chapter 2

I received a phone call from Sue, thanking me for my birth certificate and the information about my original name. She asked me if I was okay about having two names; I told her that I wasn't and explained that it had refuelled my anxiety about my lack of identity. She was phoning to arrange another appointment, and she made it clear that we could talk about it when we next met. She wanted to know more about me. I felt she was putting me to the test. She asked some questions about how I had come to terms with being adopted. Had I experienced a difficult childhood? Was I trying to get back at someone? Had I suffered in any way by over analysing the situation in my early years? Was I hiding something? And the big question: was I angry?

All I wanted to do was find out where I had come from – was that such a bad thing? She wasn't going to give anything away until she was totally clear about my motives and intentions. I think she knew that if she put me in touch with my past and I wasn't prepared, then I may do something stupid, and her job would be on the line. I am sure from our first meeting she could see that I definitely had a wild destructive streak about me.

On the day of our next appointment, Sue arrived on time again. She was wearing a long fur coat, short purple velvet dress, chunky rings and that same strong perfume. As she walked from her car to the door, it didn't look as if she was wearing anything under her coat. I was sure the neighbours thought I was having weekly meetings with a secret admirer.

I had been out very late the night before, playing at a wedding, and it had reinforced my desire to meet people who looked like me. I had stood on stage that night observing people and the similarities within families: the bride looked like her mum, brothers of the bride all had the same build, same features and a remarkable resemblance to the bride's father. Was this all getting to me? Was I becoming slightly obsessive about finding people who resembled me?

Sue sat down, declining my offer of coffee. She started to rummage through her handbag, looking for something. Her bag was full of god-knows-what. She emptied most of it out onto my table: lipsticks in all the colours of the rainbow, more make-up than a department store shop counter, a pair of stockings, keys, pens. Then, eventually, from right at the bottom of her bag, she produced a teabag – a strange green-coloured teabag, presumably herbal – and asked me for a cup of boiling water.

We sat down at last. She summarised the conversation from our last meeting and explained that she sees a lot of adoptees who want to trace their families. She went on to tell me that she always wants to know more about her clients as they usually have had a very difficult time. She needed to hear my story and asked me to start with my earliest memories as a child growing up, knowing I was adopted. And so I began to tell her the story of my childhood in Scotland.

I had a superb upbringing with very loving parents and family – some might say that I'd been a little spoilt at times. I was told that I was adopted at a very young age – I was probably three or four when my parents decided I should know. I always felt there was something unusual about me; my interior and exterior make-up was different to that of my parents. I felt like an outsider in my new family, although my parents did everything they could to make me feel wanted and loved. They didn't look like me and I just didn't have what they had – whatever that was.

Sue asked me if I thought it was too early in my life to be told I was adopted. I am not sure what the best time is to tell your son or daughter the news of their adoption, but honesty is definitely the best long-term policy. I also think there is something to be said about not ever telling a child they are adopted. (However, I do believe that any adoptee would suspect that there was something different about them.) If they are never told, they will never know, never question, never worry about it. It would have to be a big secret between the parents, though. Sue questioned me about this, saying somebody would inevitably say something sometime – a relative, a neighbour – and it would come out later. I agreed but, if you move to a new town or country where nobody knows you, you might get away with it. It would save a lot of heartache and confusion.

I told Sue about my sister. My parents had wanted to adopt again, and this time they wanted a girl. They knew the procedure, and they had already been vetted and checked out for suitability, so it didn't take long before a letter came through the post from the adoption agency informing them there was a baby girl available. I was going to have a sister.

I remember a long car journey from Scotland to London, my parents in the front, chain smoking, and little me, playing with my view master and action man in the back, staring out at the sky, seeing only the tops of buildings and trees through a smoke-filled car. The Beatles and Elvis Presley were playing on the radio. We were on our way to pick up my new little sister from a hospital in London.

I remember that day vividly. I was two years old. I recall the journey home, sitting next to a large, green carrycot, which contained a very small, crying bundle of joy. I know that I had felt a bit jealous. After all, I was the first child, and the three of us already had our set up at home. I was no longer going to be the centre of attention. I thrived on being the centre of their attention – and still do today.

As we grew up, my sister and I had great fun together – super holidays, exploring the highlands of Scotland, sitting by lochs and running through salmon-filled rivers – but the jealousy never went away. I look back at those days and wonder whether I was a good brother – I don't think I was; I was too interested in me.

Throughout those years, I wanted to talk to her about her feelings about our adoption, but she never wanted to discuss it; she always said she couldn't remember anything. Even to this day, she still doesn't want to talk about it with me.

As a child, I was given very little information about my blood parents – I don't think my parents were told much either. What I was told, however, was that my blood mother loved me very much. Looking back at that, I think it fuelled my insecurity a little and later strengthened my questioning. Why would she give me up? Why would someone give up someone they loved so much? My parents loved me very much – I knew that. Did that mean that, at some stage, they too would stop loving me and send me away? I always questioned the word love and what it meant.

It is expected that adoptees should try to forget about their blood family; they are encouraged to be grateful and thankful for their new family.

When I was young, I used to have a recurring dream of being inside my blood mother's womb. I remember feeling very much alive. I could hear. I could listen to her breathing. I could listen to her voice and her heart beat. I knew when she was drinking or eating. I could taste different flavours. I also knew she smoked. I remember quite liking it as it put me in a hazy, relaxed mood. I remember listening to music and getting thrown around all over the place, ending up upside down, then trying to move back to my usual position. I imagined she was dancing. I remember the sound of cars and buses and hearing her sing. I enjoyed the time she was asleep. I remember thinking this is my time – time for me. Dreams are funny things. I had this dream a lot; it went on for years.

I really wanted to look like my adoptive parents. Yes, I had my mother's hair colour and did resemble her a little, I suppose. But I remember how I always used to look in the mirror and be disappointed and upset about my lips. They were big and pouty, and I didn't like them. I used to spend hours folding them in with my teeth, trying to make them smaller, whilst idly watching evening television programmes with my parents. Having pouty lips seemed to be quite popular with women film stars in the 1960s, like Jane Russell, Marilyn Monroe and Lauren Bacall. But I thought it looked silly on a boy. There was Mick Jagger of the Rolling Stones, of course, but that didn't make me like them. I thought he looked like a right strange character. I thought by having big lips it would give the game away about being adopted.

I didn't really think about being adopted until I went to school and started to talk openly about it to my school friends. My parents had always told me that I was a very special boy; I was lucky because I had been chosen. I'm not sure this is a good thing to be thinking about or feeling at such a young age. I don't think it's the right thing to say to a child.

I was so proud of the word adoption, but at school it took on a whole new meaning within my peer group. I told my friends I was adopted. They went home and asked their parents what it meant and, the next day, they came back to school and told me their interpretation of what the word adoption really meant: my parents weren't my real parents, my real mother didn't love me enough or didn't want me, so she'd given me away. I have a problem with the words "real parents", and those who adopt children probably do too. It seemed everybody at school knew my predicament. I did tell people – why shouldn't I, as I was proud of it and proud of my parents.

As a child you just want to fit in; basically, you want to be the same as everyone else. Would you want your child to start wearing red trousers if the school policy is black, wear a green tie if the school colour is red? Deep inside, we adoptees wear a different uniform anyway.

At school we often had health checks. It seemed as if nurses and dentists were always coming in to examine us, give us injections, check our hair for nits and check us generally in case we had any abnormalities. I remember queuing in the huge sports hall, waiting for my turn. It was like being at a football match or a pop concert, waiting outside to buy a ticket. At last my turn came; I was at the front of the queue at the makeshift doctor's surgery. The curtains were thrown back. The doctor gave me a smile and said, "Come on in, lad, and roll your sleeves up. So, you're the adopted one?" "Yes," I replied with pride, a huge smile on my face,

At the top of all my primary school health records was the word "ADOPTED", printed in large red letters. No matter what check I was having, the medical people at school would always comment on it and watch for my reaction. Sue couldn't believe this. "That's the way it was in Scotland in the 1960s," I said.

She then asked me where I'd got my talent for music. I think she was trying to change the subject as she could see I was getting upset.

My mum had always encouraged me to express myself artistically. She was a writer, but I had shown an interest in music at a very early age – probably having listened to Dad's jazz records: Louis Armstrong, Frank Sinatra, Dean Martin, Sammy Davis and Mel Tormé, to name a few. I was introduced to various instruments at a very young age, and I was always making up music and rhythms out of anything I could find.

Sue then asked me about my dad. My father was a doctor – a GP. He was a strong and very knowledgeable man, who had great influence in the community. I liked that, but it did give me problems as an adopted child at school. I went to primary school in a small village in the south west of Scotland. We lived in one of the biggest houses in the area; we had a posh car; we always dressed in smart new clothes. We wanted for nothing, really.

I used to march to school, proud of everything I had. In the back of my mind was the thought that I was special. It was not that I was a snob or thought I was better than other people in any way. I did feel different, though. It wasn't my new shiny Clarks shoes or my pressed St Michael trousers, bought from Marks and Spencer. I knew there was something that made me different: I was adopted, and the parents I loved so much were not my real parents. In my school bag, I carried the genes of other people.

There were many traits in my personality that made me very different from my parents. I knew that I was not, and would never be, as academic as they were. I am sure that, had they had a child of their own, he or she would have been exceptionally clever. Their child would have left school with top exam results. Certificates of success were all around my house, decorating the walls: highers, A-levels, degrees, diplomas. You could say it was a little intimidating. Even at an early age, I had already worked out that I would never follow in my father's footsteps.

Going to school in the 1960s and 1970s in the south west of Scotland was very different from other parts of the country. I was constantly being asked whether I was a Protestant or a Catholic, or whether I supported Rangers or Celtic. I was a bit confused as my father was a scientific man and didn't believe in religious segregation – or even a God. He certainly didn't hold strong views on politics. Also, he was not a football fan; rugby was his thing. He'd been born in the Welsh valleys, and Wales were always at the top of the international league.

I had to think of something to say at school so I would be accepted and could blend in. I went to a Church of Scotland Sunday school, so I was probably a protestant. It was a big deal to many children, families and teachers at the time. Which one were you and which team did you support?

As a little boy growing up in that part of Scotland, it was very obvious that supporting Celtic or Rangers was very important to most, if not all, of my school contacts. It meant so much to so many people – even the teachers. It wasn't just about football; you had to be one or the other for some reason.

I remember seeing news reports of horrific violence on the terraces and on the streets of Glasgow. This was our nearest city –

only fifty miles away. Fans of both teams seemed to fight all the time. The other news story that worried and upset me was about the happenings in Northern Ireland. By the age of around eight or nine I saw the link between the two news stories: something to do with religion and class identity – otherwise known as sectarianism.

I was encouraged – almost told – by the people around me at primary school to start wearing a scarf. All the boys did. It had to be either Celtic (green and white) or Rangers (blue and white). I used to wear the Rangers scarf. Why? If I'm honest, I preferred the colour.

It was fun to be patriotic. It seemed the whole of Scotland got behind the national team, but deep down inside I knew I was not really Scottish. I wanted to be Scottish, but I'd been born in England. I used to say my mother is Scottish, but the people who knew about my adoption didn't welcome that statement. That didn't get me into their gang. I was always reminded that I had to be born there to support Scotland. I can't quite remember for sure, but I think I was the only English person at the school, or even living in the village – it certainly felt as if I was.

My parents did not fuel me at all with prejudices about anything – just basic right and wrong was good enough. It was very obvious that a lot of the kids had huge chips on their shoulders about hating Catholics or hating Protestants, and these were fuelled by bitter, prejudiced parents.

My father used to take me with him on his doctor rounds. We regularly visited community hospitals, care homes and psychiatric institutions. I would look at the people at these places and feel so lucky that I was loved, cared for and had all the right parts in the right places. These visits were so important for my perspective on life. If I were to worry or feel sorry for myself about my blood mother not loving me enough or wanting to keep me, I'd remember that these people had lots more to worry about than I ever did. These people had been taken away from their families. In some cases, their families didn't want them because they had deformities and other serious medical issues. Most boys of my generation used to read the Beano or the Dandy; I was fascinated by my father's journal, the BMJ (British Medical Journal). In it were horrific pictures of unfortunate people; it made me feel so glad to know that I was normal. I really wanted to be normal.

I have always been able to talk openly and honestly with pretty much anyone: rich, poor, needy, disabled, black or white – gift of the gab, you might call it. I really wanted to be liked; it meant a lot to me and still does to this day. I associate being adopted with feelings of abandonment and rejection; therefore, being liked and accepted by as many people as possible was, and still is, very important to me.

I feel incredibly sad when I see people with no homes and families. As a young boy I used to travel with my father and mother to medical conferences in London. I used to peer out of the car window and see pavement artists and poor street kids, begging for money. This would bring me to tears as I could have been just like them, brought up with no family or parents.

There was a film I could barely watch as a child because it upset me so much. The story line was true of so many children in the 50s and early-60s, and it could have been the story of my childhood. The film was Lionel Bart's *Oliver*. I still find it hard to watch, but it is one of my favourite films. I must have seen it hundreds of times. The songs "Boy for Sale", "Where is Love" and "As Long as He Needs Me" used to send me into floods of tears. They still do today.

I always struggled with spelling and handwriting at school. In the 1960s dyslexia was not really talked about. I don't think the word even existed; it was certainly never mentioned by teachers at school. This boy with posh parents and a mother and father whose academic qualifications were well above average was always in the bottom stream at school. I didn't like that at all. I had to sit on a desk at the front of the class. That desk was for the dunces. This was another rejection issue I had to deal with.

I was regularly beaten at school by the head teacher. He had a large two-thronged leather belt. We were made to stand upright and hold our arms out, with our palms crossed together. The teacher would throw his arms back to gain momentum and hit us three times on each hand. It used to sting for the whole day.

Why did I receive it so often? I was probably a naughty little schoolboy, who liked to show off in class to gain attention. I wasn't academic, but I would try to be liked by making my classmates laugh. In today's world it is called attention seeking.

I was far from a perfect, well-behaved child at home, too. I used to get very angry if things didn't go my way. Criticism was very difficult to take, especially if it wasn't the right reaction I wanted. I would get angry. I used to shout very hurtful words to my parents, "You can't tell me off you're not my real parents."

My parents, especially my father, could see I was having problems growing up whilst carrying the adoption banner with me everywhere I went. He recognised that I was developing an addictive and impulsive personality. Any hobby or activity I would get involved in became an obsession. I used to put so much time and passion into them. It was as if I felt the need to create the next great invention, creation and discovery.

In my spare time, I invented new board games, created school magazines, made innovative gadgets and painted wild, abstract pictures of people with no hands, ears, fingers or toes. I would write plays and stories and film them with my cine camera. I'd get all the kids in my street to act in them. I was the boss, the director, the important one.

It all sounds very flamboyant and creative but, if my ideas didn't work and people didn't like my artwork and felt my efforts were worthless, I would treat it as a personal attack, and my behaviour would become destructive – not with anyone in particular, but I would destroy my inventions and tear my work into pieces in anger.

The thrill of a new idea would give me such a high but with every high there is a low. I was very quick and impulsive with my thoughts and ideas. I would rush into things with great excitement, without really thinking them over in any great detail.

My parents sent me to a child psychiatrist. I still remember his name: Dr O`Keeffe. He diagnosed me as having an addictive personality disorder due to the trauma of having been adopted and experiencing a fear of abandonment. I was only a primary school kid and at the time I had no idea what he was talking about, but I was willing to go along with his tests. We talked about my addictions possibly being hereditary, which I thought absolutely pointless because I knew nothing about my blood parents, and it only fuelled my confusion. I had never even heard of the word. I played his silly games, making mosaics with plastic tiles, matching colours with beads, fitting wooden triangles and oblongs into a square-shaped board. I think it was called a tangram. I considered the whole counselling experience as a complete and utter waste of time.

Now, as I look back on these days today, I realise that I still have a lot of my early traits, which is a bit of a worry. If I were to sum up my memories of my early childhood days at primary school, I'd say – in my old Scot's tongue: "Ma primary skil freens and teachers saw me as the wee English adopted laddie, whose parents wurnae his real parents. He had nae passion aboot ony fitba team. He wis a posh wee bairn who lived in a big hoose. His parents had weel-respected jobs and they wur non-religious and non-political – and he wasnae any gid academically at the skil."

Sue didn't know anything about Scottish politics. She knew very little about sport, too, but she seemed interested in my stories. I continued to explain how things changed when I moved up to secondary school.

My new secondary school was okay. The thing that kept me on top form and friends with the higher academic set was sport. I was good at it: running, athletics and rugby. I was in the A-team at last. I regularly won races, which gained me credibility. On school sports days, my name was always at the top of the list of winners, and I was forever getting a mention in the local newspaper. I represented my school at running and rugby; this meant so much to me. I knew my parents thought I was great and special but, outside the family, it was important for me to be a winner and to prove to myself that I was special – different, yes, but in a positive way.

One of the drawbacks I had with sport – which probably stemmed from being adopted – was I really didn't like losing. Coming second best was not an option in my world at all. I needed that winner's medal. I needed to be the best boy at something. I needed my name at the top of the list.

Sue sat there and listened to my story. Was this what she wanted to hear, the story of a troubled child growing up? She just sat there and continued to ask me questions. She wanted to know what I did after leaving school.

I finished school when I was sixteen and immediately moved out of the family house in a rage of teenage rebellion and anger to seek my fame, fortune and identity. This was the late 70s, and I set off for London. I worked for a few companies, doing bits and pieces to get some experience, and then I moved into the creative world of the media. Being a good communicator, I naturally fell into a role where I was selling advertising space in magazines. A very popular "What's on" London entertainment magazine kept me busy. I never earned my fortune, but living in London in the late-70s was great fun. I saw some great bands and went to fabulous parties.

The punk music scene took over London at that time, with bands like The Clash and The Sex Pistols. The UK economy was in a poor shape and unemployment was running high. The youth at the time were angry and had a lot of free time on their hands to express their opinions. I was working, and I didn't feel angry in the slightest, so I didn't fall into the tartan-wearing, body-piercing world of punks. I followed the London rock scene. I was always out seeing bands like Deep Purple, Black Sabbath, AC/DC, Thin Lizzy and Led Zeppelin. I grew my hair, wore denim, lived in squats; I felt free to have a great time and forget my past.

While I was in London in the early 1980s, I was head hunted and asked to move to Brighton to help start up an exciting new arts project: a what's-on style of entertainment newspaper. We called the paper PSST. Why? Because we thought it was a good title. We published a few editions, and it was selling very well. Then, one morning, we received a solicitor's letter, telling us to stop using the name. It was from a London publishing house. They explained that there was a new lavish adult underground cartoon magazine just being launched using the name PSSST. The owner came down to see us. He was extremely charismatic and a bit wacky – a powerful French philanthropist. He ended up wining and dining us. He wanted us to change the name. He ended up buying our company for a ridiculous amount of money, and he turned our entertainment newspaper into a super glossy and extremely classy magazine.

So now our registered office was to be in London, but our publishing house was still going to be in Gloucester Road, Brighton. Every month we used to receive little white envelopes from someone living in France. We never received any explanation about them – but let's say we had so much fun for days after receiving them.

The pressure was always on whilst working for the magazine. Day and night, news stories came in about new bands, up-and-coming albums and tour dates. Promoters were always popping in, trying to bribe us with little presents to get their act on our front page. Theatres were constantly changing their show dates and, of course, we were always looking for that big news story we would work on all through the night.

I was head of advertising, but my other role was editor of the jazz section. I was always being given free tickets to the jazz clubs and events in the area. The Brighton jazz scene was thriving, and I got to meet and interview Acker Bilk, Sammy Rimmington, Cuff Billett, George Chisholm, Max Collie and the great trumpeter Alex Welsh. Alex was a big hero of mine. He didn't look well the night I interviewed him, and unfortunately he passed away four months after I met him. I also got to meet one of my all-time heroes, Chris Barber.

There was so much alcohol at these clubs, and I really got a taste for it. If you consider the fact that I was working in a candy-filled office, you can easily understand how my mental state might have taken a turn for the worst.

The office was always filled with pop personalities of the day who were performing in Brighton: Alice Cooper, The Thomson Twins, John Peel, Squeeze, Haircut 100, The Clash, to name a few – and, of course, Charlie and Henry were always hanging around. I remember being asked to review UB40 at The Brighton Centre. The day after the concert I got out my notes, but I could hardly read my writing. It said, "Someone hit something, someone strummed something, someone blew something. I can't work out which one is the lead singer." I remember thinking that day that it was perhaps time for me to consider what I was doing with my life. But, as usual, I slipped back into the same old routine the following morning.

When we put the magazine to bed (the publishing term for finishing the edition for the month), we used to head out into the shiny, seaside, veneer-coated Brighton night to look for parties. We were constantly being invited to the stately homes of the rich and famous artists in the city. They liked to invite the local press to their lavish parties and shower us with powders and painted gifts to get their stories in the next edition.

I used to walk around these houses and bump into touring pop stars, who were playing that week in the clubs and theatres. In every room you could hear the cyber jocking robojocking voices of top radio DJs, trying to impress the pretty girls. There were always long queues to the powder rooms and toilets, and that sweet smell of smoke filled the rooms, while the music of Frank Zappa bellowed though the corridors.

Inevitably the owner of the house would want to go clubbing, and we would all go to underground basement music venues to watch bands. We had two favourite clubs on the seafront, which never seemed to close. One was the Zap Club, under the Brighton arches, and the other was the Crypt, in Queens Street. The bands used to play so loud, the dead almost fell out of the walls – not so funny when your head is fuelled with adrenalin and alcohol.

Brighton was a place where you could totally indulge yourself – and we all did. A typical Saturday night would be party until the early hours of the morning, breakfast at the all-night café and sleep on the beach all day. I would often wake up and stare across the channel. I felt so rough; I was just another piece of driftwood floating on the ocean.

I was a free spirit in those days and loved it. I didn't have a care in the world; it was a dangerous, psychedelic lifestyle, but it had that excitement I was looking for.

Being very happily married now with two adorable children and responsibilities certainly puts my life into perspective. It's not just about me anymore; I have to look after myself and my family.

I have always had a slightly self-destructive side to my character, and this is something that many believe is generated by being adopted. Abandonment, wounding, yearning, trauma and separation: all very dramatic words, floating around in the adoptee's ocean.

I looked at Sue at this point. She was sitting there with her mouth wide open as she listened to my stories of my heady days in Brighton. I asked her whether this was the kind of stuff she wanted to know. She said it was exactly what she had expected as most adopted people go through a wobbly and sometimes self-harming stage. She continued, "It's going to happen to you at some stage, especially if you're not going to get the results you want from your search. You could be really hurt by this. In a way, it's good that you've already gone through it." She paused for a few seconds before adding, "Wow, you should write a book, Steve."

"Maybe one day I will," I replied.

Chapter 3

Sue sat back and took a deep breath. "Well, Steve," she said, "we must get all this paperwork completed and sent off quickly. I'm going to help you find your blood parents. Let's see if we can find you some answers to your questions. You must realise it may not turn out the way you want, and you must be strong enough to deal with the consequences we talked about." I thanked her and agreed I would try.

I had started to trust Sue. I liked her. She knew a lot about me by now, and I felt I was beginning to understand her. As part of our conversations she sometimes made comments and mentioned things that led me to believe she had a troubled life. I thought her dress sense and strong perfume were an unusual distraction for her role. On the surface she appeared to be a very sexually confident person. But beneath the painted face, short skirts, stockings and high heels, I think she was crying out to be loved. She seemed very insecure. I felt a bit sorry for her.

She explained that when she got back to the office, she would put all my reports together and send them off first class. I had to let her know when I'd heard from the court office. "Expect a reply in the next few weeks, and remember it may only be just be a letter and your original birth certificate. We can work from that, though," she said. We both stood up. I shook her hand and kissed her on the cheek. I told her I looked forward to seeing her again and thanked her for all her time so far.

I closed the door behind her and walked around the room hoping that I had done the right thing. Was I really ready for meeting up with my blood mother? I'd seen so many television programmes about this kind of thing. They all seemed to have a happy ending. What would I say to her? Would I love her instantly? Love has to be earned, surely. I could never love her in the same way or as much as I love my adoptive mother.

I remember the day the package arrived. The postman came at the usual time and knocked on the door. I could see he had a large box with a government insignia on it under his arm. He asked for my signature as a receipt. The parcel was addressed to Clive Anthony Parsons, which confused the postman. He said, "I'm sure it's not for you. The right address is on there, but you're not Parsons, are you?" "Yes," I replied, "it's a complicated story." And for the first time in my life I had to sign my original name.

I took the box indoors and put it on the living room table. Then I just stared at it for over an hour. Sue had said it would be an envelope; this was a package the size of three shoeboxes. This was the delivery I was waiting for. Was I ready? Were my emotions strong enough to handle the information inside? The box just sat there on my table in the sunlight.

I phoned my wife at work and told her of my delivery. Fearing my reaction, she said, "I wish I was with you, darling. Can you wait till I get home and we can open it together?" But I couldn't wait. I went for a walk around the garden, smoking a cigarette as if it was my last. Then I came in, sat down and opened the package very carefully. This was the paperwork I hoped would solve so many unanswered questions and lead me on my way to finding my blood parents.

The box was crammed full of loose papers – at first I thought it was packaging. They were all different sizes and had writing on them. There were also many unopened envelopes as well as a large brown envelope with a fancy seal on it. I opened the biggest envelope first. Inside was a file that smelt like an old second-hand bookshop. It was entitled Clive Anthony Parsons and had my date of birth on its binder. I still couldn't get used to being called Clive. I forced back my tears and flicked through the pages. There were some medical files and lots of handwritten letters in old, dusty, yellow-stained envelopes. There was a distinct smell about the envelopes, not just the aroma of old letters but a slight scent of perfume. It was coming from the letters and envelopes handwritten by my blood mother. This was the smell of her perfume – even after all these years.

There were so many letters. They were in my blood mother's handwriting and all were carefully signed and dated. I was seeing and touching things that she had so painfully written around the time of my adoption. I read every word on those tear-stained pages, and I could see and feel the pain she had experienced as she had written down her thoughts about giving up the baby she so clearly loved.

I now had in front of me my blood mother's name, Joyce Mabel Parsons, and my blood father's name, Geoffrey Henry Boyce. Oh, my god!

My medical records were interesting. I read about all the tests I had gone through before the adoption took place, my blood group, weight, size, polio vaccination results and dates, also my blood parents' medical records.

One of the interesting and upsetting things about reading the medical history was that I discovered that my blood father was a carrier of the disease cystic fibrosis, a disease that, in the 1960s, was quite common and extremely dangerous, especially with young children. Back in the 1960s, there was no cure. I also discovered that he had a child, a daughter, who would have been my half sister. Unfortunately, she died of cystic fibrosis when she was three and a half.

I started to worry about hereditary health problems. As an adoptee, I could never answer the local GP's questions when asked about my medical history. I could only say I was adopted. Was I now a carrier of cystic fibrosis?

I got on the phone straight away and made an appointment to see my doctor. Of course, I was concerned about myself, but I also desperately needed to know whether I had passed it on to my children. My GP understood my concern and was able to put my mind at rest. It requires both parents to carry the disease before it can be passed on. He assured me that, if I had it, I would have known something was not right by now. Even though my GP said I had nothing to worry about, I did decide to do some research into cystic fibrosis. I probably know too much about it for my own good now. He didn't want to test me; I decided to move on and not think about it.

The original court adoption records were fascinating as well as extremely moving. It gave me my birth mother's full name, her date of birth, her address at the time, her marriage separation details, work information and a long story of her life.

Now that I had her date of birth, I worked out how old she would be: eighty-nine. If she were still alive, she would probably be very frail or unwell. If I were to meet her, she would not be at her best at eighty-nine. Was I prepared to care for or financially support someone I didn't even know, even though she was my blood mother?

I had to think I would. If she was ill, I would have to care for her – I'd want to care for her. If I had to help financially, I would do that too. I couldn't just walk away. I really hadn't thought about this. I'd had a picture in my mind of meeting up with a young woman and everything being wonderful. How naïve of me.

But wait, I hadn't yet made contact. She didn't know I was looking for her; I could just do nothing, leave it like that and be content with knowing the basic information about my blood parents. I would really have to think about this. I had a wife to look after and two young children. I would be taking on a huge responsibility. Also, my parents were still alive; what would I say to them? "Sorry, Mum, I can't come over to see you very much as I'm looking after my ill original mother. You can't come and stay with us anymore as my spare room is now taken up. Oh, and by the way, do you want to meet my blood mother?" Wow, let's stop there for a moment!

There were many letters in the file and also a scruffy black book, which looked like a diary. I flicked through it. It wasn't a diary as such but a book she had used to write in. There were notes about what she was doing, how she was feeling and stories about what was happening around the time she was having me. For some reason she must have given this to the court office when she handed me over.

I had gone from knowing nothing about my blood mother to suddenly having all this information in front of me. Many of the stories were upsetting to read, but they gave me a clear picture of what it was like to be unmarried and having a baby in the 1960s. They gave me an insight into my mother's life and offered a means for me to feel the connection that I'd been looking for. It was as if she had wanted me to get to know her and understand her – and perhaps even forgive her – through discovering her pages and pages of detailed accounts, snippets of information and random scribblings. She wrote about meeting a very handsome man, who had whisked her off her feet at a hospital ball. She talked about dancing the night away and arranging to meet him again. The person she was talking about was a man called Geoff, my blood father.

He is a doctor, a very fine, good-looking, respectable man with caring, sympathetic eyes. He can dance very well and treats me like a lady. I have fallen in love with this man called Geoff. He tells me he is married. So am I, but separated. We have a lot of fun together. We meet at weekends and go dancing to the big bands in London. It is inevitable we are going to spend the night together – we both want to.

We had a great evening last night at the Hammersmith Palais, listening and dancing to Joe Loss and his Orchestra. We booked into a small guesthouse called The Blue Vanguard and finally had sex. It was amazing!

Why have I included this in my writing? Well, I presume if she wrote this down in her book she wanted someone to know about it, so I was conceived after a night out, dancing to one of the great jazz bands of the era – nice!

Geoff spends the weekdays with his wife. He told me that they had a daughter, but she sadly died and his wife can't and won't have any more children. He was very fond of her and is very sad that she has died.

It is December 1960. I have just found out I am pregnant.

The next page of her book was very sad.

I stood on the doorstep of the doctor's surgery today, eyes glazed and staring into the busy crowded Stanwell High Street. I have just realised my life will never be the same again. Three girls walked by in very short miniskirts and brightly coloured hats. They were holding a radio, laughing, giggling and singing along to Adam Faith's "Someone Else's Baby". I was sure they turned the radio volume full up as they got nearer to me. I used to like that song; not any more. A man in a top hat with a cane smiled and asked if I was okay. I tried to smile back politely, but I was crying. My face felt like it was made of hard plastic and wouldn't respond. I held on tightly to the railings of the surgery entrance. This morning my doctor confirmed that I am pregnant.

The bus ride home seemed to last forever. I looked out of the window; all I could see – or wanted to look at – were ladies with their husbands pushing prams. I am terrified about telling my parents my news.

I want and need to tell Geoff, but I am not seeing him till next week and have no way of contacting him. I don't want to tell

Teddy, although I am still legally married to him. I think he is still commissioned abroad.

Teddy must have been the name of Joyce's husband.

I went home today and, as I arrived and opened the door, my mum stared at me as she knew something was wrong, very wrong. Her eyes are always very welcoming when I come home – not this time. She said, "You're pregnant, aren't you! What the bloody hell have you done?" She knew I was dating Geoff and probably knew I was sleeping with him.

I ran upstairs to my room in floods of tears and slammed the door. Moments later there was a knock at the door, and my mother was screaming at me to pack my bags, get out of her house and never return. The thuds on the staircase as she ran downstairs shook the pictures in my room. I heard her scream, "Just you wait till your father comes home. How could you do this – bring shame on the family."

It seemed like minutes, but it was well over an hour before I heard the pounding of the stairs again. The door burst open. It was my father shouting, "Get that bastard child out of my house. Leave tonight and don't tell anyone about this, do you hear me?"

I am being allowed to stay tonight, and I am frightened. Tomorrow I have to leave; I don't know where to go. I can't sleep, and all I can hear are my parents shouting and arguing downstairs.

It's 6am. I'm sitting in a cafe with my suitcase, pad and pen. I feel totally alone. People keep staring at me. The world is walking by outside and I don't feel part of it anymore. The only thing I can see is my sad reflection staring back at me in the window. How long can I make this pot of tea last? I walked the streets most of the night and slept rough in a derelict garage in Hadrian Way. I must look terrible; I am in no state to go into work today.

This morning I am going to take a bus ride into the centre of London. I worked last year as a make-up model for a top agency in Carnaby Street. I am going to seek refuge and advice from my old boyfriend at the agency, Tom. I know Carnaby Street very well. It has always been the top spot of the UK fashion scene. I did very well there for a while. I know Tom; hopefully, he'll help me. After all, I was one of his top models.

I have just been to my old work place, where I saw Tom. What a bloody waste of time he is. I walked up many stairs passing open doors with scantily dressed women counting money, and, as I approached the office, I was pushed aside by men running down the stairs adjusting their ties. I knocked on the glass window of the agency office door to be greeted by my old, so-called friend, Tom. He said I looked terrible. I probably did as the last time he saw me he was taking pictures of me in long posh dresses and I was wearing full make-up. I stood in the doorway, in unwashed ragged clothes and in tears. I told him I was pregnant and needed help. His only remark was that I should get rid of it, smarten myself up and never come here again. He told me they don't need girls like me here. He then looked round the hall to see if anybody was watching and slammed the door in my face.

I couldn't wait to see Geoff and tell him the news. He is the only one left who can help me. I think he might be pleased. He said his marriage was going through a difficult time because they couldn't have any more children. He might leave her and have the baby with me.

Yesterday the doctor said there is a place I can go. He wrote the name on a scrap of paper. I have it here. It is called Red Gables: a mother and baby home in Crouch End. I am going today. I have nowhere else to go.

I have just been to Red Gables. I knocked on their door, and a lady answered asking what I wanted. I explained to her I was pregnant and had nowhere else to go. I was welcomed in today and given a cup of tea and showed round and told I had to have a written letter from my doctor and register with social services to be allowed to stay there. All my letters are going to my parents' house in Bedford Road and Geoff is going to meet me there in a couple of days. I have no other choice; I have to go back home and try to sort this out.

If Joyce wasn't happy about having the baby, why didn't she have an abortion? Also, why hadn't she and Geoff used contraception? I started to research.

There was no female pill or morning-after pill in these days. Yes, there was a very basic male condom available, but most men didn't know how to get them. But this was the fab 1960s, the sexual revolution, a time for free love – which basically meant sex without protection, I suppose. Some people say if you remember the sixties you weren't there.

Having an abortion in the early sixties was illegal; it was practised by back-street, so-called doctors, midwives and struck-off foreign medics in filthy conditions. Disease and death were a common occurrence. You could go to dodgy doctors in Harley Street and pay lots of money in used bank notes, but even then you were never guaranteed good health afterwards.

It used to cost between £100 and £150 – a lot of money in those days. I found out in my records that Geoff's salary was only £625 a year. The people carrying out these procedures were likely to face a prison sentence of five to ten years, especially if the pregnant woman died. Geoff couldn't justify losing that amount of money, to his wife anyway.

The most common advice at the time for getting rid of an unwanted pregnancy was gin and a really hot bath. Many women never knew how much gin to have or how hot the bath should be. This is just one of the reasons why gin is called "mother's ruin". There was other advice going round – horrific suggestions such as trying to fall down the stairs a few times or putting hat pins inside yourself – but I don't think Joyce wanted to get rid of me or contemplated any of these options at all.

Chapter 4

By reading Joyce's letters and looking at her notebook, I was learning very quickly about her life at the time of the pregnancy. There was nothing about her childhood, family or marriage in my files; it was as if she wanted someone – perhaps me – to know what actually happened during that period in her life. I imagine someone at the adoption agency or court had told her that all the paperwork to do with the adoption would be kept in a file forever and the only person who would be authorised to see it would be her son – me.

Turning the pages and reading her handwritten accounts of that period was so hard. Nobody seemed to care about single unmarried women who fell pregnant in the early 60s. It is so different nowadays as the government really looks after pregnant girls, giving them homes, support and benefits. Back then you were on your own – totally on your own.

Joyce had some thinking to do.

I am back at my parents' house, sitting upstairs in my old room. I have been told to keep the curtains drawn and not to look out of the window. The bulb has been taken out of my light, and I'm using a candle to see. I had to come back home; there is no other way. I can't believe they are prepared to disown me. I never got on with them that well; my sister was always their favourite. My mother is a drunk, an alcoholic. She is a musician and plays piano. She is hardly ever in as she plays all over London. I think she's good at what she does; she certainly gets lots of work. As a young girl I used to go with her and listen to her play. I was sure sometimes she didn't get paid proper money. The owners of the clubs would just buy her drinks all the time. She would take me home in such a state.

If it weren't for my dad, I wouldn't be here tonight. He talked mum into it. They have given me a few days to sort things out. I am constantly told of how ashamed and disappointed they are in me. I even have to eat supper in my room. We also have new rules: I have to leave in the morning for work when it is dark and come back late so none of the neighbours can see me. I have also been told not to mention the baby or my pregnancy to anyone. It is nice to have a hot bath and feel clean again.

So Joyce's mother was a musician – fascinating. I wonder if I got my talent from her. I was playing with a lot of the top British jazz musicians around the time of my searching: Norman Thatcher, Brian Carrick, Derek Winters, to name a few. They were a lot older than me and probably played in the jazz clubs and dance halls in and around London in the 1960s. Norman Thatcher used to play with Ken Colyer and Acker Bilk. They were big names around that time. I wonder if Joyce in her dancing days ever went to see any of them play.

I visited my doctor today. I quite like him. He is the only one who listens to me these days, and he is sympathetic. I think he sees hundreds of women like me. It is just nice to talk to someone normal without all the arguing and shouting. He has given me a referral letter to apply to stay at Red Gables. He said they would sort out the social services paperwork while I was there. I am seeing Geoff tomorrow. Maybe everything will be okay.

I am not feeling very well. I am constantly being sick, my work has suffered and today my bosses have put two and two together and I have been sacked from both jobs. Now I am faced with having no home and no job. I have very little money, and the prospect of bringing up a baby on my own seems impossible.

Geoff came round today. It was so good to put on a nice colourful dress, put my make-up on and have my hair done. I had not been to the hairdresser's in such a long time. We went out to a local restaurant. I was so pleased to see him but very nervous about telling him the news. He knew something was wrong as soon as I got into his car, as I didn't have on my usual happy, bubbly smile when I saw him. He was not angry in the slightest. He was shocked, though. He is a logical thinking man and sat me down with a large glass of wine and we talked. He is not prepared to leave his wife. He said he still loves her and, although they are going through a difficult time, they are staying together. My heart dropped. He is such a nice man; I probably don't deserve him. We talked about Red Gables. He is a medical man and works in various hospitals around the area, so he had heard of the place. We also talked about what he was going to say to his wife. Then he mentioned the idea of having our baby adopted.

I started to research mother and baby homes in an around London and soon came up with the name Red Gables. Seeing pictures of the house that Joyce and I stayed in was emotionally upsetting but interesting.

Red Gables was a beautiful Victorian house in Haslemere Road, Crouch End, London. It was formerly an orphanage and had been used to provide mother and children's services of one kind or another since the Second World War. It closed in 2005. The local Haringey council had been threatening its closure for many years, sparking anger from over 600 spirited campaigners to try to keep it open. It was put on and off the market by estate agents with a price tag of £1.2m in 2012. The local residents association was worried that the council would sell the land to a developer who planned to knock down the building and turn it into flats. The building itself holds many memories for so many people; it would have been a shame to see it turned into profit for the council. I found out it was saved and is now Crouch End

Nursery and Playschool. I have just talked to the head teacher there. She described it as a fantastic, well-respected place, where the children are so happy. Apparently it still has the original big garden, just as it was when it was Red Gables. She also mentioned that some of the dads who bring their children there were adopted and born at Red Gables. I left my number and email address. You never know, they may get in contact.

> I have had to come to terms with Geoff not wanting to marry me and be with me. He also cannot help me look after the baby, as, although his wages are good, he really does not want to commit himself. He also said if he did help me, his wife would find out there was money missing from his account. I felt like saying it was our responsibility but the words just would not come out. He also told me he was not going to tell his wife anything about the baby.

> We decided today that our baby needs to have two parents. This is something we strongly agree on. If we can find the right couple it will be for the best. We both think adoption is the only answer.

Nowadays it is very different to look back and understand the terrible wrench and barbaric act of separating a mother and child just because they are unsupported by an uncaring society. In the 1960s, the stigma of illegitimacy was such that many young women were more or less forced to give up their babies. They were expected to go away to a mother and baby home, have the baby, and then just hand it over. Unfortunately, this was a similar story for thousands of women at this time.

> Geoff and I went to Red Gables this afternoon. I had the authorised letter from my doctor with me and was expecting to be told to come back in a week or so, but they took me in straight away. Geoff was not allowed in. We said our goodbyes,

45

and he arranged to pick up my things from home and drop them round later.

There were some letters in my old dusty files from various authorities saying Joyce, aged thirty-nine, had been admitted to Red Gables, where she would have time to think about the future of her baby. I had so much information about Joyce's life in that file from the court. It just made me cry and feel so sad. Those letters were written at a time that must have been so hard for her.

I'm staying at Red Gables now. I have been told that adoption would give my baby both a mother and a father and a home full of nice things – things that I would not be able to provide. With no support at all from my family it would be virtually impossible for me to bring up my baby and support myself financially or find suitable accommodation. Even if I had money, no establishment would want a single mum and a baby staying at their house.

Joyce's notes were fascinating to read. She wrote openly about life in the mother and baby home. It seems hard to comprehend how difficult it really was, especially comparing it with how things are done today. I did a little research on the subject and discovered that there were over 170 of these types of establishments in England during that period. Adoption reached its peak in 1968, when the total figure was 16,164. That's a lot of babies who need parents.

There are 14 of us in the home. We all get on reasonably well. I suppose we are all in the same predicament. I am a lot older than all of the girls here and the only one who is married. Of course, I am separated, but I am reminded every day that I am not married to the father of my child. I suppose I am more experienced in life than the rest. In fact, I am older than some of the nurses and staff.

Matron is forever telling us that we are very lucky because this is a home for good girls, but, if we get pregnant again, we should never expect to come back here. She tells us that some homes are nothing like this. They are like prisons, run by not very nice people. If we get in this situation again, we shall find ourselves in one of these places, mixing with prostitutes and street girls.

The matron here at Red Gables is a sympathetic lady of sorts, cold in appearance but deep down I know she has a job to do and very rarely shows us any emotion.

Our routine is the same every day. We are woken at 7 o'clock by matron knocking on our door. I share a room with five other girls. Every day, I have to strip wash in a basin with a screen around me. There are four screens to a bathroom. There is a large pool in one room where some of the girls bathe together. I do not like to do that. Sometimes I book the single private bath in advance. Matron keeps a list on her wall, and, being the oldest, I get first turn every time.

Once washed and dressed I go downstairs for breakfast at 8 o'clock. We all sit at a long wooden table, eating disgusting porridge and cold toast, chatting about our partners. We have a list given to us – matron is very strict about this. It is called our chores. Our chores depend on our condition, that is, how long we have left before we are ready to give birth. It has nothing to do with our health. The ones with a longer wait have the biggest job list. We do help each other, though. As long as all the jobs at the home are done by the end of the day matron is happy.

I, along with some of the other girls, scrub the floors everyday. The stairway is always the most difficult to do and the most painstaking. Matron inspects that first. If it isn't good enough we have to do it again. We are constantly fetching buckets of coal for the many open fires in the house, and we also have the main boiler, which needs topping up all the time and is right at the top of the building.

If you are not on coal duty, you are on water duty. Buckets of hot water are being used every hour for cleaning, cooking, washing and topping up that huge bloody boiler.

If the girls are coming very close to having their babies, they are put on either washing or cooking duties, or else they get to prepare the babies' bottles. And if they feel ill, they are given sewing and mending work to do while in bed.

Matron says the chores are part of our punishment and a way of paying for our stay. Most of us do not mind doing them, as it means that the time passes more quickly. We are also told that scrubbing the floors on our hands and knees keeps our muscles supple, which will make giving birth easier.

We also have to feed the babies. This is the best job. It starts at 5.30 in the morning and goes on in shifts until 11 o'clock at night. Mothers are never allowed to feed their own babies – that is the rule. They tell us that contact with our own baby is restricted to prevent us from growing too attached to our child. Matron tells us that we must not get too emotionally close. New mothers are never allowed to breast-feed. Instead, they use a pump and put the milk in a bottle. Then another mum feeds their baby. I don't like the idea of breast-feeding, anyway. Sometimes they give the girls tablets and medicine to stop their breast milk.

By about 3 o'clock our chores are over and we are allowed to go to the rest room, a large room with around 20 chairs. It has a huge bay window overlooking the garden. We sit and chat and play games. I am good at cards; we played all the time when I lived in Egypt.

Okay, that was a new one to me. So, Joyce used to live in Egypt. The plot thickens! I wondered if she was married there and that's where her husband lived.

Gambling with money isn't allowed, so we use our cigarettes. I win most times but share the cigarettes around. We sit in the rest room, smoking, knitting and playing cards. Sometimes, if the weather is nice and matron is in a good mood, we are allowed to go for a walk into town, where we can have tea and go shopping.

On Tuesday and Friday afternoons we are allowed visitors. Not many of the girls have visitors – nobody wants to know them, especially their parents or partners. I am lucky as Geoff comes to visit me. He always brings me cake, biscuits or a pie. We go for walks in the park, visit a nice tearoom and chat about the future of our baby. I always knew Geoff would never leave his wife; he has always been very clear on that. We talk openly about the adoption.

We both get on very well. He is very different to me – he is a straight-talking, practical man. I like him and would marry him if he asked. He would have been good for me. I am always flustering over things and making things a lot bigger than they actually are. I have been called a drama queen many times in my life.

If there is anything that needs repairing at Red Gables, Geoff always offers to fix it. He spends hours here sometimes. God knows where his wife thinks he is. He always has a screwdriver in his pocket or a hammer in his hands and tools in his car.

We have weekly visits from some of the midwives from the local hospital. They are totally focussed on preparing us to give birth and never have time to explain it properly or talk about anything else. We are never offered any help with emotional issues at all. They always seem so busy and never stay long.

On Sundays we are all marched down to the local church. We do have an option not to go, but I go, as I believe in God. Everybody knows where we are from and the looks we get from some people and the comments shouted at us are horrid. "You shouldn't be going to church. You're all sinners and sluts!" is a common one. We are all told to sit at the back of the church so that we do not offend or embarrass other churchgoers. Those of us who are close to having our babies are allowed a seat, and the new mothers have to kneel.

We spend a lot of our time preparing baby boxes. We are all asked to find a plain box from the local shops and write our name on it. A lot of the girls use false names to hide their identity. We have to decorate the box – either paint it or stick colourful paper on it. We are told that our boxes will travel with our babies. The box will be given to the new parents. I never told the other girls, but I found lots of boxes in a cupboard one day. They were filled with knitted clothes and letters. There was never any intention of giving the box up with the baby. I didn't bother doing one. I decided not to tell the other girls about what I had found.

As soon as a new mother comes back to the home with her baby, we are all dying to ask what happened and how she got on. A lot of the time their waters break while doing a chore and matron or a member of staff just hand out nappies and say, "You're nearly ready. Stick this in your pants while we get the car."

We are never really told much about the birth process and most of the girls come back with horrendous stories about having been in so much pain. I don't think our girls are given any pain relief at all. They all come back the same day in tears.

We have social workers who call on us before and after the birth. They explain the adoption process, but, to be quite honest, they never stay that long and most of the girls do not understand what they are saying as they always have other things on their minds and other places to go and always talk so quickly. I am lucky as Geoff explains everything to me. He is very good at that. Both of us are clear about what is going to happen and when. I have spent a lot of time nursing in Egypt and have helped deliver a few babies, so I can explain to the other girls what to expect. Most of my time in the forces was spent nursing wounded soldiers, but I knew a bit about babies.

In my files it did say something about Joyce's background and occupations: "Separated nine years ago, no children, worked as a shorthand typist, then as a demonstrator and model for make-up. Nursed in services during the war. Married abroad. Since separation has worked as a receptionist and does welfare work. Some nursing WVS." It did make me sad to think that after all the things Joyce had gone through she ended up in a type of workhouse baby factory for "naughty ladies".

I do feel sorry for two of the girls. They have mixed-race babies. Nobody wants to help them in any way, as people do not want to adopt coloured babies. The staff at the home do not spend time with them, either. They just sit by themselves, not saying very much and never joining in. The members of staff have told them that no one will want their babies. I think they will be forced to go back home. I don't know what's going to happen to them. We are told that girls are easier to put up for adoption than boys because men have problems coming to terms with having a son who does not have their genetic pattern. We were also told that boys are going to be more trouble.

I like to think that Joyce did use her knowledge, wisdom and experience to help the other girls get through a very difficult time, both emotionally and physically. It is difficult to understand how a woman must feel when she is pregnant, about to give birth, and then going to be forced to give up her newborn baby. The journey through pregnancy, to birth, to adoption must be crammed with feelings of shame, happiness, guilt, joy, sorrow and a whole host of other unnatural mental acrobatics a woman has to feel – the numbness, overwhelming pain, more numbness and eventually submission is overwhelming to think about.

Matron keeps a box of cheap, gold-coloured rings of various sizes in her drawer. She calls them her secret jewels. The girls are given a ring to place on their wedding finger just before going into hospital to give birth. This provides an element of dignity for the girls as it allows them to appear to the other mums and hospital staff as if they are married. Matron tells us that some hospital staff and a lot of the other mums-to-be will look down on us, even bully us, because we are having our babies out of wedlock. A gold ring on our left hand stops any judgment and hurtful comments. The girls always hand them back when they come back to the home, having had their babies.

Joyce mentioned in her notes that she still wore her wedding ring all the time. It sounded as if she was still legally married but separated. She talked about receiving a separation allowance. I wondered why she was separated and what had happened? The next pages of her writing I found very hard to take in.

Matron has talked about the humiliation that the girls are subjected to whilst in hospital. I want to know what she's on about. I am older and wiser than the other girls here, and I would like to think I am a thicker-skinned. I have no shameful story to tell about how I got pregnant and, if someone is going to launch into an argument or confront me, I am ready for it. My waters have just broken and I have just taken my wedding ring off and put it in my drawer. It makes me so mad how the girls are treated here.

Geoff and I have already decided that it is best if I go into hospital on my own to have the baby. He does not know I am going there today. I am not going to write anymore until after the baby is born. Today is the 30th of July, 1961.

Well, I am home now, and all I can say is I have had the worst experience of my life. I was driven in a taxi to Edmonton Hospital, where I was greeted by the reception staff. I was asked where my husband was, and I told them I was on my own. I could see their expressions change. They showed me to the maternity unit and gave me a bed. There were six other beds on the ward all filled with pregnant ladies. Before I changed into the hospital clothes, I introduced myself to the others. "Hello, my name is Joyce. I think we are all here for the same reason, girls."

One of the ladies noticed I wasn't wearing a wedding ring and shouted at me, "Are you one of the whores from over the road?" I stared at her and said, "What did you call me?" She replied, "You're not wearing a ring. You're obviously not married, are you? Bloody disgusting."

I would have liked to have answered her back, but I started to feel a bit embarrassed. I had been taken off guard. Besides, I was not feeling very strong that day. I sat on my bed and started to cry. A nurse came, and I was taken to another ward for an examination. I could not stop thinking about the words the lady had said to me.

It was obvious that the ladies in my ward had been talking about me while I was out of the room. When I returned they all laughed and stared at me. My bed sheets had been thrown onto the floor, and my bed was all ruffled up. My pillows were lying on the other side of the room, and my suitcase had been opened. I shouted at them and asked who had done this. They all started to laugh again, and one lady shouted that she hoped I would bleed and miscarry. That was it; I had had enough. I stormed off and found a nurse, and I told her what had happened. We both sat down in the corridor. She listened and apologised, and then she said, "But this does happen often to women in your predicament." I replied, "My predicament? But I'm just here to have my baby."

She told me I was from the home, and I asked her how she knew that. "Well," she said, "you're not wearing a wedding ring, so I presume you've come from Red Gables." "Yes," I replied. She explained that some of the married women who come to the hospital do not like Red Gables; they think it is a bad, sinful place, and they pick on the girls who come from there.

The nurse apologised, saying that there was not a lot she could do. I told her I had worked overseas in many hospitals as a WVS nurse. She paused and asked me to wait in the corridor. I didn't wait. Instead, I walked straight back into the ward and gave them a mouthful. "You know nothing about me or my baby." I swore at them and told them I had been married for years and that they knew nothing.

The nurse returned and helped me pick up all my things, which were, by now, all over the ward floor, including my suitcase. I think she took sympathy on me as I was older than her, and she now knew about my nursing experience. I could hear the ladies in the ward giggling and talking amongst themselves. One of them shouted down the corridor that I was a whore and that she hoped my bastard baby would die.

The nurse told me to follow her. We walked through the corridors, listening to screams coming from behind closed doors. We then arrived at a blue door. She opened it and said, "If you keep your mouth shut and don't mention Red Gables, you can have this room." I agreed. She then said, "But you'll have to wear a wedding ring. I know where there is one." I agreed that I would and thanked her for being so kind. I will never forget that nurse.

I was given my own room with a lovely view over Pymmes Park. I unpacked my suitcase, carefully refolded my clothes and changed into the hospital gown. I had a picture of Geoff with me, so I put it on my bedside cupboard. The nurse returned and gave me a ring to wear. It was a bit tight, but I managed to get it on. I asked her for her name. She replied, "Just call me sister – that's fine." I thanked her again.

Sister came to check me regularly. Even the night staff were friendly. Was it all down to me having a ring on my finger and a picture of the father of my child by my bedside? I was keeping it on, for sure. Every nurse asked where my husband was and would he be in to see me. I decided to pretend Geoff and I were married and told them he had to go abroad on medical business. I had known Geoff for two years, so I could talk about him quite easily.

I had my baby at 10.45am on the 31st of July, 1961. It was a forceps delivery. I can't believe I am saying it, but I am so pleased to be back at Red Gables with my son.

Chapter 5

Joyce stayed overnight at the hospital and returned to Red Gables with me on 1 August 1961. We both stayed there for six weeks. She had obviously continued to write her notes, but now, for some reason, they were on scrappy bits of paper, all different sizes. They were written using various colours of pens and pencils. Some of her notes were quite difficult to read.

> If what I experienced in hospital is anything to go by, women in my situation were blatantly bullied and ganged up on when they should have had a natural relaxed birth. We have our own worries about giving our babies up and the last thing we need is naive bastards trying to make us feel even worse than we do already. I now understand why matron keeps her secret box of rings and tells us to wear them.

I don't know why Joyce didn't wear her wedding ring in hospital. Had she done so, she would have had an easier time and been a lot more relaxed, comfortable and better treated. Well, I know this sounds hard, but she chose to experience what it was like being an unmarried pregnant woman in those hard uncaring times. Maybe she didn't want to wear her husband's old wedding ring for sentimental reasons, but that doesn't follow, as she wore it most of the time anyway. I think my blood mother was a bit of a rebel and wanted to test the system. Perhaps she was also a bit of an exhibitionist. She had mentioned in her letters that she was a drama queen – not sure I feel comfortable about that. I think I carry more of Billie's genes than I realise!

> I am back at Red Gables with my baby boy. He is so beautiful, and I am so proud of him. I wish I could keep him forever. I know

the Red Gables' rules, so he has to go into the nursery with the other babies, and I am not allowed to feed him or spend a lot of time with him.

Geoff is arriving today. I am really looking forward to seeing him. We have been told not to go out anywhere, so I think we will just sit in the garden.

Geoff came to see me today. He was so pleased it was a boy. He held him and I could see that he would have made a great dad. I did suggest we could keep him and change our minds, but he said we had to stick to our plan, and adoption was the only way. I know he is never going to leave his wife, but I had to try again. We had to think of a name today. We have decided to call him Clive, and we both agreed he would take my surname. He is adamant a boy needs a father. We talked about it a lot and I agreed. He brought some adoption paperwork with him that we both had to sign. I didn't read it. I just signed.

I have that form they both signed that day. It was amongst the paperwork I was given by the courts. It was one of the few forms that had my blood father's name on it.

It seems that, by law, we are not allowed to look after our babies ourselves in the home during this first six weeks after giving birth. This, they say, can encourage a bonding process that is not good for us or our babies. What a load of rubbish – it is only six weeks. We are not allowed to sleep in the same room as our babies, nor are we allowed to breast-feed. I have been given the pills to stop my milk.

All our babies are kept in the nursery under close watch by the staff. The cots are all labelled with our names. We are allowed to carry out the very basic kind of care for our own babies, but, generally, we are put back to work and given chores to do. One day I am washing all the babies' clothes, the next I am changing all the babies' nappies. That chore gives me a little more time with Clive. We are treated a bit like work skivvies here – washing, scrubbing floors, cleaning the kitchen. We are kept busy all the time, but it is probably a good thing.

I have been given the opportunity a few times to take Clive out into the garden. Matron said it is a reward for my extra help with the other girls. Geoff was here today. He is interested in photography and he took some pictures of Clive and me. I asked him if he wanted me to take a picture of him holding our baby, but he did not think that was a good idea. I did not understand why.

Another one of Joyce's letters I found upsetting to read was a story of one of the girls she met at Red Gables. I have changed the name of the girl.

What a day today has been! Last night, one of the girls at the home, Teresa, managed somehow to take her baby out of the nursing room. She has gone. No one can find her. I think she may have changed her mind about having her baby adopted. There is panic here this morning, and the staff are going crazy. Red Gables is not a prison – you can come and go whenever you want to a certain extent – but if the baby is up for adoption and the paperwork has been signed, you are told to stick to the rules.

There are frantic phone calls being made and people are rushing around everywhere. A police car arrived in the driveway this afternoon, and a man in uniform came to the door. We were all watching at the windows. He didn't stay long. We have been told to stay in our rooms today and wait for the supper bell. I'm not sure the matrons would even recognise the baby from being at Red Gables. It is all very formal here, and probably the only one who could recognise the baby would be Teresa.

We have just been down for supper and shown the local evening paper headline: "Baby found in a telephone box." We are all in shock and feel frightened for Teresa and her baby. We do not know for sure that it is hers, but we think it is. The staff at the home are very quiet and hardly speaking to us. We have been told to go to bed early tonight. The girls in my room are talking about going for a walk tomorrow morning to see if they can find Teresa. I will go too.

We have just come back for lunch. We all went in different directions for our walks and tried to find as many telephone boxes as we could. There was one two streets away, in Christchurch Road, with a policeman outside it. One of our girls tried to talk to him. She asked if there was anything left in the telephone box that she could recognise as being Teresa's. The policeman just said he could not talk about it.

The evening newspaper has just arrived and is covering the story on the front page. They are appealing to the locals for information and for the baby's mother to come forward. It also said that the baby is fine and at the local hospital.

Today Teresa came back to Red Gables and there are a lot of policemen here. Her baby is back too. She told us this evening that she is confused. She hated being pregnant and hated giving birth. She does not want the baby as it is a reminder that she was raped. We explained to her that the adoption would be quick and the best option for both her and her baby. The police have decided not to press charges. I am just glad they are both safe.

I received a letter from the adoption agency today saying there is a couple interested in adopting Clive. I have been given very little information, apart from they live in London and have a big garden. They are married and cannot have children of their own. The man is a doctor. I like that. Clive should be able to have a good life and be well educated.

I still hate the idea of being separated from him, but there is nothing I can do. It has been almost six weeks now, and I have to leave Red Gables and go back home. Clive is going to stay with a foster mother until all the legal paperwork has been done. It is reassuring that I can visit him.

I read on, and her words reduced me to tears, yet again.

I feel a bit like a tortured soul. I have treasured every moment I have had with Clive. I have been told to try to forget the baby and make a fresh start. I have told the staff that is something I will never do. I know I cannot offer Clive all the things he deserves. I am so sad.

This made me even more determined to try to find her and thank her, not only for the adoption but also for not having me illegally aborted. I needed to thank her for living with the heart-wrenching choice she had to make in giving me up for a better life.

During the time when Joyce was looking after me at Red Gables, there was a reference in my medical notes, saying that I quite often discovered a sound that I would repeat over and over again. Fuck, this is something I still do privately to this day when I'm at home – much to the annoyance of my family. I just catch an interesting resonating word or phrase and play around with it with my voice. It is very similar to what a vocal coach would make you do. It's also a bit like jazz scatting. So, I started doing that when only a few months old and still do it – how amazing.

As the mothers were coming up to the end of their six weeks at the home, Joyce noticed the devastating effect it was having on them as mother and baby were spit up.

I have got to know many of the girls here in the home, and I can still hear their screams echoing through the corridors as their babies were being taken away. It is a daily occurrence. Saturday is the busiest day of the week for collecting babies as most people have jobs and work Monday to Friday. Saturdays have become known as "Sadurdays".

The care workers come in the middle of the night. They dress the babies and take them from the nursery downstairs to reception. We hear the cars and can see their lights, as they pull up at all times of the night. The cries of those babies will haunt me for the rest of my life. The girls do not even know which babies are actually being taken that day. The next morning they are heartbroken when they discover their babies have gone and they have not had a chance to say goodbye. The days after the separation are the worst. I talk to many of them about their pain. Some of the girls contemplate suicide. Thank goodness none of the ones I've got to know ever do. I am one of the lucky ones; I know where and when my baby is going.

Today Clive is going to stay with the foster mother. I had a chance to meet her and talk to her yesterday. Her name is Mrs Blake. She seems okay. We exchanged addresses and filled in lots of paperwork.

This afternoon Mrs Blake took Clive. It was very hard, but I knew I would be seeing him in a few days.

Geoff picked me up in his car yesterday. I said my goodbyes to Red Gables. We drove straight to a bar, and I got really drunk. I was in no state to go home to my parents, so we stayed the night in our usual guesthouse.

Today Geoff dropped me of at my parents' house in Bedford Road. They were expecting me as Geoff had dropped them a note saying when I would be home. I told them what happened and *what I had done. I really wanted a big cuddle and their reassurance that I had done the right thing. However, my mother refuses to discuss anything and I have been told to pretend nothing has happened and never to mention it again. Does my punishment fit my crime? I do not think so.*

In the files, there was a court letter, which stated that, before adoption could take place, the child had to have a surname registered. In addition, they would have to contact Joyce's husband for consent. Joyce kept her married name even though she had been separated for nine years. Her maiden name was Oram. Joyce never wanted this to happen because she didn't want her husband to know about the baby, but the authorities tracked him down and he was told the news. As a result, Joyce lost all her separation allowance and became completely penniless.

Reading through the file and letters was interesting, painful and extremely difficult to comprehend. As I turned the pages, I read more and more information about my birth, the legal adoption, court details, etc. I then came across a form entitled The National Adoption Society, confidential application in respect of a child for whom adoption is sought. In it, I started to read about my blood father. The form described him as a man Joyce had met a couple of years prior to my birth at a hospital ball. Once again, my tears started.

Section 15/16 gave details of the full name, age, nationality and last known address of the child's father. My jaw fell open. He was called Geoff Henry Boyce, aged 38 – a year younger than Joyce. The form describes Geoff as a Head Occupational Therapist, earning £625 per annum. Nationality: English. Height: 5ft 7.5in. Colouring: olive. Hair: dark brown. Eyes: blue. Interesting features: nice looking, quiet with sympathetic eyes.

So, if Geoff was only 5ft 7in and Joyce was 5ft 4in, I wondered how I had ended up 5ft 11in. It seems I have my father's hair and complexion and my mother's hazel eyes.

Section 6 of the form was also interesting: "Has either parent of this child had any other children? If so, state age and sex." The details stated: "Father, yes. Daughter aged three years and one month." Was I now to believe I had a half sister out there? Then I remembered that in Joyce's letters I had discovered that Geoff's daughter had died.

Joyce's interesting features on the page were stated as: "Very thin, hard-looking woman, artistically inclined, likes dancing, hair brown but dyed blonde".

So I least I had a rough picture in my head of what they both looked like and could compare myself to them a little.

There was a letter written by the Children's Officer of Kent County Council, describing how Mrs Parsons and Geoff Boyce brought the baby to their office on 19 October 1961. The baby was introduced to his new prospective parents. Under strict instructions the parents of the baby were not to meet the new couple adopting the baby. This was obviously my first meeting with my parents formally.

Another letter from the same council sent to Joyce's address stated that on 2 November 1961 Joyce was asked to pick up the baby from Mrs Blake's house and bring the baby to the office with his medical card, the welfare food books, a list of his diet and routine, a tin of food, a parcel of his clothes and nappies and a prepared feed. It would be the last time she would see him. Joyce writes:

> This is the saddest day of my life. Parting with my beautiful baby is the hardest thing I have ever had to do. I really don't want to lose him. My heart is broken. I will never be the same again and will always think of him. I will never forget him.

Today the agency gave me a bottle of holy water and a set of rosary beads. What an exchange! I am so sad.

The day I read all of these notes, letters and files I must have gone through three packets of cigarettes and drunk eight or ten cups of coffee. That night, I finished off a full bottle of whisky and cried myself to sleep.

There were a few more letters from Joyce to the adoption agency during December of 1961. She wrote and told them her doctor had admitted her to a mental institution suffering from severe depression, and she was asking the agency if she could send me a Christmas present, a soft toy. The letters back to her stated they don't normally do this kind of thing but if she was to send it to the agency with the postage costs they would pass it on. She was given strict instructions not to enclose a letter with it.

The agency did forward the parcel on as I remember I had received a cuddly panda on my first Christmas. My parents had told me it was from somebody very special. I loved that panda. It was always my favourite comfort toy, and I kept it for many years.

There are copies of letters my parents sent to Joyce via the agency thanking her for the present, updating her on my progress and news and they enclosed a picture of me lying on a rug as a baby for her to keep. I thought that was lovely and very kind of my parents.

I had gone through my life wondering what happened, and why, and how my mother could give me away if she so-called loved me so much – how can you love someone then just toss them to one side. Now I know, she didn't toss me anywhere. To quote Joyce: "I want my baby to have a family, a mother and especially a father. I want him to have a happy childhood with loving parents and a good education. I am very pleased he will be brought up in a doctor's home, full of the nice things that I could never give him. I will always love him and will think about him every day for the rest of my life."

Joyce was admitted to a psychiatric hospital two months after I was handed over to my new parents. In her doctor's report in my file, it states that she was suffering from a nervous illness and hysteria. His reason for advising that she be institutionalised was because of her erratic, strange and uncontrollable behaviour. Also in his report, the doctor said she was weak, was having headaches and was showing alcohol dependency.

Joyce still wrote while she was in hospital but her handwriting is almost illegible. She talks of being hot and cold: "They give me four cold showers a day. They say I'm depressed. Being in here is hell. I am taking medicine, and I sleep a lot. I don't know what they are giving me."

There are lots of bits of paper with little drawings on them, not of anything tangible, just lots of circles, small ones over large ones. There are also childlike drawings resembling babies. She starts a sentence then just puts a long squiggle after it. It is heart-breaking to see them.

Chapter 6

From reading Joyce's letters and notes, I have learned so much about the adoption process and what it was like to be a single pregnant woman in the 1960s. It was very obviously a difficult time for young pregnant women, who found themselves in the situation where they were having babies without the stability of marriage and without monetary support.

Most, if not all, of the women were forced to give up their babies, and adoption was the only way forward for them. Back then the government did not support single parents. They did not encourage unmarried women to keep their babies; in fact, it was frowned upon. The stigma of illegitimacy and carrying a bastard baby was around everywhere.

The Church of England insisted that girls keep their babies for six weeks. This would give them a bond with the child that was later to be taken away, and the pregnancy itself would add a further nine months to the bonding time period. It wasn't just Joyce's parents who insisted on giving up the child; most, if not all, parents around at that time would have said that the baby would have to go – mostly through embarrassment and shame of what others might think. This situation was the norm. If the girls refused to give up their babies, they would only be threatened by the system to attend mental institutions until they finally had to give in. I wonder if any parents of unmarried mothers still alive today regret the painful decision of forcing their daughters to give up their children.

Many of the girls had affairs with men working in the forces. Later, they would discover that the men were already married and wanted nothing to do with a baby; they had simply enjoyed the comfort of a young woman's tender warmth and companionship whilst they were so far from home. On hearing the news, the soldiers often requested a transfer to another part of the country or even abroad – long gone, never to be seen again. Many of them didn't even tell the girls their real names.

It was not all about the military men, though. Lots of couples were irresponsible and ill prepared. I would like to think ill informed – but, come on, we all know how babies are made. What do you get from free love? A free child. As I had just discovered, I was the result of an evening spent dancing the night away to one of the top jazz bands in the world and a late night romantic meal with a bottle or two of fine wine, before going back to a nice warm guest house for a night of passionate, unprotected sex.

A few days after the package arrived from the court, I went into town on the bus to do some shopping. I couldn't stop thinking of the letters and notes that Joyce had so painstakingly written. The bus was filled with young girls with babies and toddlers, running up and down the aisle, shouting and screaming. The mums did not seem to be very interested in stopping them; they were either chatting on the phone or having an in-depth conversation with a friend.

When we reached the final stop in the centre of town, I politely sat there and let them all off the bus first. They were manoeuvring pushchairs and holding on to the seat in front of me for stability. I couldn't help notice that most, if not all, had no wedding or engagement rings on.

That morning, I ended up walking round town in a bit of a daze. I found myself looking at girls pushing prams, pushchairs and buggies and staring at girls holding the hands of toddlers. I was wearing sunglasses that day so it wasn't too obvious that I was watching them. I started to count how many of them were not wearing a ring on the third finger of their left hand. It was quite easy as most of them had their hands exposed pushing the pram. Very soon I lost count. I couldn't believe how many of them, presumably, were not married. It was not something I'd ever noticed before – or even cared about – but after the last couple of days of reading about Joyce's predicament, I had started to think about how much things had changed over the years: young women's expectations, society's acceptance.

I continued with my day in town, buying things on my shopping list, standing in queues waiting to be served, still doing my little survey in my head. Were they married or were they not married? I started to wonder about the story each one of them had to tell about their situation. Did they have partners? I began to feel sorry for the children. I would have loved to know for sure, but naïvely I presumed that they were all mistakes – stupid, I know.

I thought this is crazy; why am I getting so interested in what other people are doing with their lives? It's none of my business – and I was far from perfect. But what was at the forefront of my mind was this would not have happened in the 1960s, only fifty years ago. Back then those confident, happy girls I had been observing whilst I was shopping would have been intimidated, shouted at, verbally abused, bullied and probably not even been served in shops. And more importantly, if they were not married and had no money, they would not have been allowed to keep their babies.

That same day, I bumped into a friend, who lives in my village – I say friend, but I knew her as the girlfriend of a musician I used to play with. She had fallen pregnant many years ago – she must have been around sixteen at the time. My musician friend wasn't the father but befriended her for a few years, and I got to know her reasonably well.

I was walking into a wine bar for lunch when she came up to me in the doorway and asked if she could join me. I really wanted to be on my own that day but said okay. I have changed her name in the story; I am going to call her Sally.

Sally fell pregnant when she was a teenager and has never worked a day in her life. She lives in a nice council-owned, two-bedroomed house in my village. She is now thirty-six years old,

68

and it's common knowledge in the village that she receives a lot of benefits. That day she looked a bit low and confused. I offered her a seat at my table and bought her a drink. I had a coffee, and she asked for a glass of wine.

She ended up telling me her life story that afternoon and, over the second glass of wine, started to tell me in a very blasé way why she had never had a job. She explained it was pointless working because of the benefits system. She went on to say her sixteen-year-old daughter was seven months pregnant. I knew her daughter from afar. I watched her grow up in the village. She used to walk up and down my road. She just seemed a little girl to me. How time flies.

I think she was expecting me to be excited and happy for her. She obviously didn't know what was going on in my world at that moment, and I wasn't going to tell her. I congratulated her on the fact that she would soon be a grandmother. I was polite and acknowledged her joyful news. But I knew I had done so in an artificial way. I smiled in all the right places as I drank my coffee and listened to her story.

Sally told me she was so pleased her daughter was pregnant and would help her get all the support she herself had received over the years. "It's so easy, you know," she said.

I listened and watched my friend's personality change over several glasses of wine. She started to get slightly angry, agitated and a little aggressive. She told me how her daughter had gone to a party, got drunk and spent the night with a boy. At that point I nearly walked away, eyebrows raised. But, no, I wanted more – this was interesting.

She went on to tell me her daughter hadn't done very well at school, so being pregnant was a great way for her to avoid working in a shop or a department store for next to nothing. "She is going to work the system – like me," she went on. "Other people will pay; why should she. It was just a mistake. We all make mistakes, don't we?"

I nodded in the right places again. Bloody hell, I was a good actor that day. I was fuming inside. At this point, I actually considered telling her about my findings, but I stopped myself; I didn't know her that well and could see that this was going to be a one-way conversation. I just listened. She continued. "She's already on the housing list, and we've seen pictures of a possible new home for her, but we have to wait till the baby is born."

I asked Sally about the father of her daughter's new child. She snapped at me. "Look, as far as everybody is concerned, he walked out on her, and we don't know where he is."

I asked again. This time I got the real answer. "Well, he's still around, and they're still together. He's a nice enough lad, but they haven't known each other that long. He hasn't got a job and still lives with his mum. If they tell people they're together, they won't get a house and all the other support. She's going to have a better life this way. He hasn't got any money anyway."

I must admit I did feel slightly angry inside. Had Joyce, my blood mother, lived today, she would have had all these perks. There would have been a new home for her and me; she would have been looked after financially. There was no such system back then. Sally mentioned her daughter was going to have a better life. Joyce had been told that I would have a better life by being given up for adoption and living with other people.

Like a red rag to a bull, I asked Sally if her daughter had considered giving her child up for adopted. Well, I can't write the words that came out of Sally's mouth at that moment, but it was basically along the lines of, "You are joking! F***ing adoption! That's for drug addicts, alcoholics and losers who can't look after their kids. We are going to have this baby and work things out together."

My acting skills were way on form that day. I just sat quietly and listened. I had already started writing Joyce's story. I had been going through her letters and scraps of paper, trying to piece things together in a logical manner. I was hoping to get more information at my next visit with Sue, my adoption manager. I wanted to do more research into the whole concept of adoption. Research! Here it was; I just had to listen and pay attention to what Sally was saying. These were the real life, current day details, and I was being fed them over several glasses of wine.

"We're going to do this together," Sally said. "I know exactly how the system works. It's the government's fault for giving us all this money and encouraging us to have children and not to work. Do you know, she'll get more money than most of her friends that work get, and she'll be the only one who has her own house. Most of her friends can't afford their own place and are still living with their parents." She also went on to say how the government was giving all these immigrants homes and money to stay in this country, and that it was time that we got our share.

I may be very old fashioned or naïve, and my mind at the moment is bitter and sad about Joyce and her life story, but why should the government pay for your daughter's alcohol-fuelled mistake, and why are you encouraging it? I didn't say that, of course. I kept my thoughts to myself. As she was recounting this, Sally didn't know I was adopted – she had no clue about my story. One day, she may read my book. Will she recognise herself in my story even though I have changed her name? I think she will.

We ended our little chat by me saying I had to meet someone, and we left it like that. I felt so annoyed. Who was I annoyed with – Sally, her daughter or the system, who knows? I certainly didn't like her attitude to adoption.

As I travelled back home on the bus that day, I wondered whether being adopted and discovering all this information about what it was like in the 60s had made me over sensitive to the single mum issue and children needing to be with both parents. Times have changed, but it was barbaric of the government at the time for insisting women had to give up their babies.

When I got home, I thought about the conversation I'd had with Sally. It made me wonder just how many single mums there were and why they were on their own. What had gone wrong? I started to do a little research on my computer and was shocked by my findings.

According to a recent report from the Office for National Statistics (ONS), there are approximately two million single-parent families in Britain. Women account for ninety-one per cent of these. So, the vast majority of these children are being raised in a household where there is no father. I think that is desperately sad. The office also states that just over one in four families is now led by a single parent and that Britain is the European leader when it comes to children being raised by a lone parent.

I wanted to know why these statistics were so high. It seems the reasons fall into four categories:

1. Generation Gap – young adults have a different set of moral values and beliefs regarding sex, marriage and raising children than previous generations.
2. Divorce – The traditional family home with a mother and father is no longer the norm as divorce rates continue to rise. Some feel divorce is better for the children when parents are very unhappy with each other.
3. Unplanned Pregnancy – this seems to fall into the younger population mostly and blames the lack of maturity and a decreased desire for further education and careers.
4. Choice – many women choose to have children by using a sperm donor because they simply have not found the right person to marry.

Well, as far as point 2 is concerned, the older generation would say the youngsters of today don't work hard enough at marriage. There are always ups and downs in a relationship – good and bad times – and it is too easy these days to give up. I must admit, I have heard that so many times before in radio discussions about this very subject.

The ONS statistic stating how one in four families is led by a single parent was brought home to me years ago, when I used to take my children to primary school. I was one of very few dads in the playground – and one of the very few dads attending the school concerts, plays, fêtes and sports days.

I never got a father's day card made at school by my children. When I asked the head teacher why that was, I was told that they didn't want to upset the children who didn't have fathers, so they didn't encourage the children to make them.

By doing a bit more research on websites and exploring the social media on this subject, it did become apparent that the stories of girls like Sally and her daughter getting pregnant just to manipulate the system for financial gain are not as common as they are made out to be in the media. It certainly seemed like it talking to Sally, but thank goodness it is not the norm.

So why are so many girls falling into the single parent statistics? Some girls talk about feeling pressured by their partner into having sex without any protection; partners tell them they can't feel full enjoyment wearing a rubber mask, and the girls feel embarrassed to insist they wear one, especially if their partners are older, which seems to be very common. Others say they genuinely didn't think it would happen to them and they just get caught up in the moment. The pill didn't work, the sheath broke or they blame their partner, saying it wasn't on properly. And the most common one that I found on the Internet's social network sites: "I was pissed."

I am very aware of the social pressures on young girls today. They are constantly being fed sexual images: in advertising, in the media and in pop videos. There are images all over the place portraying sexual activities. I sit in doctors' and dentists' waiting rooms reading women's magazines, and I see it all. Come on, doctors and dentists, let's have more sports and fast car mags in your waiting rooms, please!

I believe that when single girls find out they are pregnant, they do have a decision, or an option, if they are not sure or ready to take on the responsibility of a child. It is the biggest decision they probably have ever had to make. They could have it aborted – unlike in Joyce's day. Abortion was illegal in the 1960s – thank god, as I may not be here now. Please, let me be clear, I don't have a view on abortion. It is an extremely controversial subject, but the option is available free on the NHS in the UK. Many girls have very dominating mothers, like Sally, who are likely to discourage their daughters from taking this option as they feel it is either dirty, unethical or an easy way out – my words not Sally's. Poor Sally, I keep mentioning her, but it was an interesting lunchtime conversation.

The other option the girls have is to have the baby adopted. Now I do feel strongly about adoption as I think it's a wonderful thing and if a woman really feels she can't look after the baby, bring it up in a loving way or afford to keep it, give it nice things with a good education the best option is give it to someone who can. But I think that, in today's society, adoption is an option that youngsters are not going to take very often because parents are much more supportive and understanding these days. They are willing to help more – and, dare I say it, they are absolutely over the moon and perhaps even selfishly excited about becoming a grandparent.

Chapter 7

So I had my blood mother's name, date of birth and her address at the time of my birth. I knew she had been married to someone called Teddy. They got married and lived in Egypt, but they separated nine years before Joyce fell pregnant. She was working out there as a WVS (Women's Voluntary Service) nurse in service during the war.

So, if she was thirty-nine in 1961 (when she gave birth to me) and she and Teddy had been separated for nine years, that would make her thirty years old when she left her husband. I guessed that she had probably left the forces in 1952.

I had a quick look through the military services archives of the activities and personnel in Egypt from 1940 to 1952. Google images had pictures of lots of WVS ladies working there at that time. Was I looking at a picture of Joyce? I found a Teddy Parsons who was stationed in Cairo, Egypt, around that time. He was a chief leading airman, who gained much recognition for his flying skills and was highly thought of by his higher-ranking officers. But I wasn't looking for Teddy and didn't want to spend much of my time tracking him down; it was Joyce I was looking for.

I needed to talk to my adoption rep again. All this information (facts, figures, dates and stories) was – to put it bluntly – doing my head in. I became aware that I was smoking and drinking far too much; it was really starting to affect me mentally. I knew nothing about searching for long-lost ancestors or family connections. Had I simply been trying to complete my family tree, like any normal person might do, I think I would have found it less emotional. Here I was, getting my hopes up, fantasising about ladies in uniform in Egypt, scrolling through military records and telephone directories looking for the name Parsons. It was all getting a bit too much on my own.

Thank god I am a jazz musician because going out most nights and playing is so therapeutic. I found myself getting lost in my music. The old standards became symphonies. Playing and singing the blues became painfully authentic. My fingers bled and the blood dripped onto my double bass. If I were going a bit crazy, there was no better place to be than standing on a stage, singing and playing in a jazz band. I was able to escape and become totally immersed in the music. But then I would get home very late at night, hit the bottle and it would all come back to me.

I needed to see Sue again, so I made an early morning appointment. This time I went to her office. The walls in her office were covered in photographs and newspaper cuttings of adoption reunions: daughter standing with mother, son in the arms of father, pictures of smiling sisters who had only just met. It was a bit intimidating. There was also a wall filled with, what looked like, adverts. The one I will always remember stated, in big bold letters: "Little Toby is looking for a new mum and dad. Can you help?" The poster had a picture of him playing on a bike, and he looked so sad.

Sue was interested to hear what I'd discovered so far and told me I was very lucky to have found so much information. She also said I was to take confidence knowing that Joyce loved me and wanted me to have a good, loving home. I was hoping Sue could use all this new information to help me find my blood mother. She reminded me how old Joyce would be now. She prepared me for finding her name on the death records and the possibility of never meeting her.

We started to look at a website called The Adoption Contact Register. This is a site where, if your blood mother or father wanted to get in contact with you, they could register their name with the site. Then, if you put your details in, there would be an instant match – bingo! This is the only way a mother or a father of an adopted child can express an interest in a reunion as it is impossible – in fact, illegal – for them to search for their birth son or daughter.

We tried it, but there was nothing to be found there. Considering most people in their eighties don't use a computer, I wasn't too surprised at that one.

We continued the search, but we were coming up with blanks. Birth, marriage and death records gave us no information. I knew Joyce was married, but had she perhaps moved back to live in Egypt? If that was the case, it wouldn't come up on the UK sites. She may have got married again in the UK and changed her name. If she had changed her name, what had she changed it to? Possibly back to her maiden name? I was pleased there was nothing coming up on the UK death records. That gave me hope.

Sue and I looked at hundreds of Parsons in telephone directories and electoral roles, but still we came up with nothing. Having her date of birth helped us to search, but there was still no record of her. We tried to find a list of ladies who had stayed at Red Gables. That information was confidential, and we came up with nothing again.

At lunchtime Sue encouraged me to go to the local library and ask there. She explained that they might have access to international records, which were not available to us. A kind lady at the library took my information, and we sat down to look at pages and pages of old blue microfiche records. The only thing we found were some details from a ship's boarding register. It was from the 1970s, and the ship was heading for India. It gave details of a woman with the same name and birth year, who was travelling with a boy. I knew Joyce had lived in Egypt with her husband, so she would have been used to a foreign lifestyle. Did she now live abroad? Did I have a half brother? If either of these scenarios was correct, my search was going to get harder.

That afternoon, I went back to Sue's office and told her what I had found. She explained that, if it was going to be an international search, then her contacts were not going to work because she could cast her nets in the UK only. She recommended that I get in touch with a charity organisation called AAA-NORCAP (Adults Affected by Adoption). The way it works is you pay them a fee and they do their best to search for your missing relatives. It is a bit like a private investigation bureau with contacts all over the world.

NORCAP (the National Organisation for the Counselling of Adoptees and Parents) was established in 1982. It offers practical support and services, advice and counselling to adults whose lives have been affected by adoption. In particular, it works with adults who want to obtain information about their birth family or have renewed contact with birth relatives and need guidance and help.

The service is used to ensure contact is made in an appropriate manner and that each person has adequate support at, what can be, a very emotional time for everybody. According to the NORCAP figures, some four million adults in the UK live with the impact of adoption.

I signed up, paid their fee and registered with NORCAP. I saw this as an investment into my inquisitive and increasingly desperate search. I filled in all their paperwork, provided the relevant information and photocopied everything I had that might possibly help. And then I waited.

Back home I carried on searching. It seemed as if I was constantly on the Internet, putting surnames into any site I thought would give me information. I researched the address Joyce was living at when she went to Red Gables, only to find the whole street had been knocked down thirty years previously. I was determined to find her. Joyce's stories had left me feeling sad and scarred, and I was compelled to thank this woman for her courage.

The last piece of writing I read from Joyce was about her being forcibly admitted to a mental institution. Had she ever recovered?

I couldn't bear the thought of her dying in a place like that, with depression and a broken heart – all because of me.

One late Friday afternoon I received an email from NORCAP. Unfortunately, I didn't keep a copy of the email, but this is roughly what it said:

Dear Steve,

We have traced your blood mother, Joyce Mabel Parsons, and it is with regret we have to inform you that she passed away two years ago. We enclose the death certificate as an attachment.

The researcher dealing with your search will, unfortunately, be on holiday for the next three weeks. She will be in touch with you on her return.

Regards,
(Name withheld)
NORCAP

Fuck, she's dead! Fuck, I am two years too late!

Although I had been warned by both Sue and my mother about this possible outcome, it made no difference to the sadness and grief I felt. I poured myself a very large whisky and then sat back and sobbed my little heart out.

It was devastating to hear Joyce had passed away – and to make things worse I was only two years too late with my search. This was why she wasn't appearing on the death register; it was not up-to-date on the Internet (or wasn't at the time of my search). Seemingly, it was two years behind as it takes so long to register everybody's deaths on the national site. NORCAP, however, had access to up-to-date records.

NORCAP had said they would be in contact when my researcher was back from holiday. Well, I certainly couldn't wait three weeks for more information. I now had a copy of the original death certificate, and I knew where the death had been registered. It was Brighton, a place where I had lived for many years. Reading further down the page, I found her home address – a flat in Stanford Road, Brighton. I used to live in Dyke Road, in Brighton, just around the corner – probably less than a minute's bloody walk from her flat! I walked down Stanford Road almost every day on the way to the centre of Brighton. I noticed, too, that her maiden name, Oram, was given as a sub-heading. She had kept her married name Parsons for all these years. There were also details of another name she used, a nickname. She was known as Billie.

I had never known any girls called Billie before. Brighton was, and still is, a very cosmopolitan city. Was my birth mother bisexual or gay? She had never remarried. The name Billie suggested to me she was possibly gay.

The certificate also said she had been cremated. I realised that I would never have a place where I could go to visit her and pay my respects. Yes, I could go to see a book of condolence, but that is not the same in my view. I wanted to meet her, hold her hand and say thank you – or at least visit her grave.

I contacted all the hospitals in Brighton, hoping for more details of her death or people who knew her. The certificate said she had died of a bladder carcinoma, atrial fibrillation and frailty in old age. I drafted an email. Then I copied it, pasted it and sent it to all the NHS residences in and around Brighton. Some of the hospitals responded, saying how sad it was to hear my news but they had no records of a death of someone with that name at their establishment.

Having lived in Brighton, I was familiar with the local newspaper, *The Argus*. I searched online, reading through all the archived obituary columns, every entry from the day she died to almost a year after. This was a time-consuming task as *The Argus* is a daily newspaper. There was no record of her death. I found nothing.

Next, I decided to contact all the funeral directors in and around Brighton, hoping to find the company that had dealt with her funeral. This was a long shot, but I needed to go down every avenue. It was another lengthy task. I emailed about twenty of them, asking if they had dealt with the service. I told them I was a member of the family.

A week or so later I received an email from a secretary at a company called Arka Funerals, in Brighton, explaining they had arranged the service and funeral.

On the death certificate I had received from NORCAP, there was the name of a person who was an informant. I didn't know what an informant was. The informant's name was Penelope M. B. I wanted to know who she was and what she knew about Joyce. I discovered that an informant is a person who formally provides information about the deceased (such as full name, date of birth, place of birth, last address, etc.) to the death registration office. It is usually done by a member of the deceased's family.

I had Penelope's surname, and it wasn't the same as Joyce's (or Billie's). Was this Joyce's girlfriend or partner?

I wrote to Acorn Funerals again, thanking them for the information. I enclosed a more detailed letter explaining who I was and why I needed more information. I heard nothing so I decided to phone.

I spoke to a female member of their staff, who said she remembered the day very well. Apparently, there had been no family there at all – which she had thought strange – just lots of her friends. They had released ten white doves into the park; she'd had a white coffin and a white hearse. She said she would never forget the day because as the doves were released there was a very strange eerie feeling in the office. The windows had flown open and the sound of birds' wings flapping had been deafening. All the computers had stopped working and the lights kept flashing on and off. "Yes, it was a strange day," she said. "I think one of the guests said she had been a spiritualist."

I asked her why there had been no family, but she didn't know. This made me feel very sad; Joyce had died and no one from her family was there to say goodbye. Surely her family were not still angry with her about having had a baby out of wedlock. That had been nearly fifty years ago. The eerie feeling she talked about made no sense to me at all.

I then asked the lady from Arka about Penelope, the informant. I wanted to know who she was and why her name was on the death certificate. The lady was very secretive about that and refused to give me any information; however, she did say if I wrote a letter to them, she would pass it on to Penelope. Of course, I understood the confidentiality surrounding the situation. After all, these people had never heard of me. Perhaps they thought I was looking for a family inheritance or something.

That day I wrote a letter. And, again, it was time to wait. I hate waiting, but there was nothing else I could do.

My letter was worded sympathetically; I chose my words carefully, offering my condolences to Penelope. I then went on to explain why I was writing the letter. I described a little bit about my research. Then I added the bombshell words: she was my mother!

All this recently discovered information was fucking my head up. I knew it was getting to me emotionally, and I needed to offload and share my thoughts, feelings and findings again. I realised I was getting way out of my psychological comfort zone; my anxiety and stress levels were sky high. I was happy, had a great loving family, was enjoying bringing up my boys, loved my music and band – so, why did I want more? Why was I asking so many questions? I always want more; it's one of the hang-ups of being adopted, I think. Was I now pushing myself too far?

I phoned my mother – as she had asked me to keep her in the loop – and told her that I had found Joyce but she was already dead. Mum was very sympathetic and said, "Well, you can stop searching now and move on. I hope it has answered your questions. You don't have to be obsessed with it anymore." I think she had been talking to my wife; she knew this was important to me, but she also knew I wasn't coping very well and that I'd been getting very upset and involved – over involved in my mother's eyes.

It was time for me to get in contact with my adoption rep again. Sue came round to the house a few days later. She knew I was having problems taking in all the information, and she realised that it was upsetting me. She listened attentively to my recent findings. I think she could feel the anger and frustration in my voice, knowing that I'd been two years too late in finding Joyce. She helped me take in the fact that I would never meet Joyce and explained to me it would take me time to get over it. She explained that it would be like going through a period of mourning.

She was right. She explained the five stages of grief that I would go through:

1. Denial – the shock of discovering Joyce had died was hard, but I found comfort and peace in pretending it had never happened, that the whole search never happened. A few glasses of scotch in the evenings helped forget things, for sure.

2. Anger – yes, I was angry. I started my search too late. I felt guilty as I could have found her ten or twenty years ago and enjoyed getting to know her. I felt no anger with anyone else but myself.

3. Bargaining – if only I had done this whole thing years earlier. If only the system allowed the blood mother to make contact with the adopted child, she may have tried to contact me.

4. Depression – this one speaks for itself; I was feeling low and helpless.
5. Acceptance – I was allowing myself to feel grief, even enjoying feeling the grief at times. I'd never experienced anyone very close to me dying before. I was a jazz/blues musician and singer, and this would give me the opportunity not only to sing about pain but also to feel it in the lyrics.

Sue directed me to the present. "In your original court files we have the name of your blood father. Could he still be alive, do you think? Let's have a look at that."

So much emphasis is placed on the search for the blood mothers, which is understandable, I suppose, as they are the ones who went through pregnancy and birth. Joyce – or Billie as she was called – was dead, but my blood father may still be alive.

I knew his name, his occupation, his age, and I had an address. He would also be well into his eighties. Once again, I had to be prepared to confront an elderly man and possibly disrupt his peaceful, happy, aging world with my selfish, self-centred search for answers.

I told Sue I had written to a lady called Penelope, a sole name on the death certificate, and had sent the letter to the funeral directors. She told me not to get my hopes up; if there had been no family at the funeral, Penelope would probably just be a neighbour or a nurse at the hospital or care home and wouldn't know too much about Joyce.

Chapter 8

I had just got back from playing at a funeral – my jazz band plays all types of gigs. When playing at the funeral of a jazz fan or musician, we typically walk/parade in front of the hearse or horse and carriage, playing dirges and spirituals, as the mourners follow on behind. We play again in the church and then afterwards, at the wake, where we play more uplifting music to celebrate the deceased's life. The custom is based on a New Orleans style of funeral. We have a video on YouTube of that particular day's event. I paraded that day in my special military parade jacket, top hat, white gloves and cane. All the time I was thinking of Joyce's funeral with its white doves, white coffin, white hearse and no bloody family. I looked around me as we played; so many people looked like each other. It was obvious that there were loads of family members attending this funeral. I was still very upset that Joyce's family had not come to her funeral. I just couldn't work out why none of them had come. I came to the same conclusion as before: it had been my fault.

When I got home the phone rang. It was a lady asking to speak to me. She said her name was Penny. It didn't mean anything to me, so I asked who she was. She said, "You wrote to me through Arka Funerals. I've just got your letter." I replied, "You're Penelope?" She asked me to call her Penny and went on to explain that Billie had been her best friend. They had known one another for thirty years. She told me she knew all about me as Billie had talked about me all the time.

I found this hard to take in, but I was pleased. I had to ask her, first of all, why Joyce had called herself Billie. Penny explained that it was because she was a bit of a tomboy at school and her friends used to call her Billie the Kid from the film of the same name. Apparently, the name just stuck. "So she wasn't gay then?"

I asked. Penny laughed and replied, "Oh, no, far from it. She loved being with men."

Penny seemed really friendly and chatty. I think she was genuinely excited that she was speaking to me. She kept saying, "I can't believe I'm talking to Billie's kid." She started to call me Clive. I suppose that's the name Billie used when she talked about me. I asked Penny politely to call me Steve.

She told me that Billie used to carry a photograph of me everywhere. After the adoption, my parents had sent her a picture of me lying on a rug in my new home. She kept it in her purse and was with her everywhere she went. Unfortunately, Billie's handbag had been stolen while she was in the local supermarket; she was devastated when she lost the photograph. Penny said she had seen that photograph so many times. I told her I knew about the photo. I had lots of information given to me by the court office that handled my adoption, and it is mentioned in there that my parents gave it to her.

I also told her I'd been given a box full of things relating to my adoption from the court office: handwritten letters and notes from Joyce during the time she was pregnant. Penny said, "I have a big box of things for you too. I collected up all her personal belongings after the funeral and kept them, hoping one day you would get in contact."

Penny asked me to refer to Joyce as Billie because, apparently, she had never liked the name Joyce. I was curious to know whether Billie had had any more children; she hadn't.

I explained to Penny that I knew Brighton well as I used to live there. I said, "She used to live in Stanwell Street, didn't she?"

"Yes," Penny replied.

"I used to live in Dyke Road."

"I know that road very well," she remarked. "It's just round the corner from Stanwell."

"I know. I lived and worked in Brighton twenty-five years ago."

"Well, Billie was there then, so you could have seen her walking down the road." I thought it was interesting that Penny mentioned that; I had already thought about it too.

I had to ask her why none of Billie's family attended her funeral. I said that the lady at Arka Funerals had mentioned it. Penny explained, "Well, I'm afraid Billie never forgave her parents and family for insisting she give up her baby, kicking her out of the house and not supporting her. She just never kept in contact with them; she felt very bitter about them." She went on, "It's so sad that Billie has died. I really miss her. She was the maid-of-honour at my wedding. We have a lot in common, Steve. I was adopted as well, you know."

I asked Penny her age. She replied, "I'm the same age as you. Billie and I used to joke about it."

Penny knew so much about Billie. As she said, she was her best friend and had known her for thirty years. She went on to say, "Do you want to see pictures of her?"

My heart stopped. "Wow, yes, please!" She asked for my email address and said she would send some over to me that night.

Penny said, "I really hoped you'd make contact one day. I must scan those photographs for you. You'll be so excited to see them." We must have talked for over an hour. We ended the call both knowing we would speak again very soon.

This was definitely a time for a large whisky. I had just talked to my blood mother's best friend. I had so many questions for her that I'd forgotten to ask. But at least I was starting to get to know a bit more about her adult life. Thank god she pulled her life together and got away from that terrible mental institution.

That night I just stared at my computer for ages, pressing refresh on my inbox every few minutes. I didn't move from my chair until her emails started to come through.

Sure enough, Penny's pictures of Billie's life over the years started coming in. There were pictures of her as a young woman right through to her elderly years just before she died: Billie as a young girl in a smart RAF uniform, Billie as a glamorous model, Billie as a young and very attractive woman in a stunning dress with Teddy at her wedding in Egypt, Billie holding me as a baby in the garden at Red Gables, Billie as a middle-aged woman at various social gatherings – including her as the maid-of-honour at Penny's wedding – right up to her elderly years, fundraising at charity events. The picture of Billie and me at Red Gables had obviously been taken by Geoff. She had mentioned it in her diary. Was this what my searching was all about – seeing hard copy proof that I had a birth mother?

At first, seeing those pictures gave me an overwhelming feeling of guilt and shame. I now had pictures in my house of two mothers: my real mum, hanging on the wall next to Dad, and my blood mother, on my computer screen. What the hell had I done? I think the term for this is the "adoption triad". This was a real head spinner. Time for another drink, I think, and a walk round the garden in the dark.

I imagine my children got a bit confused seeing the photographs. There it was right in front of them – the facts. Their grandmother – the one they loved so much – wasn't their real grandmother. My dad wasn't their real grandfather. My sister wasn't their real auntie, and her children weren't their real cousins. They had many other relatives on my side of the family. Were these relationships now also in doubt? They knew the situation, but this was bringing it home big style, and I could see that it was upsetting them.

I started to feel guilty about my search now. It had felt right, but now it felt wrong. I felt so close to my real parents that evening. I just wanted to phone them and tell them I loved them very much. But I was in no emotional state to talk to anyone that night, apart from my family at home. I was also starting to slur my words due to the whisky.

I stared at the photographs and tried so hard to see a resemblance. For some reason, it didn't hit me first time; I really wanted it to. I found it so emotional seeing her at last. She was a very beautiful woman in her early years – a real stunner – but seeing her old and frail was not so good. I think most adoptees imagine their blood mothers to be young women. One thing I noticed though was her lips. She had those big pouty lips I had so despised as a child – big, round and very distinctive. Whatever I had done all those years ago as a young child – such as folding them behind my teeth for months on end – had worked; I certainly didn't have lips like Billie anymore.

That evening, I sent off one of the pictures – possibly taken when Billie was roughly the same age as I am now – to some of my friends. I couldn't see a resemblance. I wanted to know if my friends could. They all saw it instantly, even the ones who didn't know about my searching. Some of them said she had my eyes; others said she had my facial features, and that, for me, it should be like looking in the mirror.

I was really excited now, and I wanted to share my news and findings. The following day, for some stupid reason, I forwarded the pictures on to my mother with a note saying: "These are pictures of my blood mother, Billie."

What was I doing? What was I expecting? I was excited; I thought she might be too. I wanted to share my news with my mummy, the one I had shared my life with so far, the one who had brought me up, had shared ups and downs with me. What was I thinking? This was going to be a direct kick in the teeth.

Over the phone, she calmly said, "They are very nice. She was a very pretty woman."

"But, Mum," I asked, "can you see a resemblance to my blood mother?" Yes, I know, I had just kicked her in the face, and now I was going for a headlock by asking her to notice a resemblance. She simply replied, "You may not have my eyes or smile, Stephen, but, from the moment I met you, you had my heart. A mother is someone who raises you, tucks you in at night, takes care of you when you're sick, guides you, teaches you morals and values and protects you – remember that."

Then I asked her whether she liked the one taken in the garden at Red Gables. So, I'd done the facial damage, and Mum's head was in a headlock. I was now going for the final punch: showing her a photograph of her little baby boy in the arms of another woman. What the fuck was I thinking of? Oh, yes – me, me, me again!

She said she didn't think it was me in the picture, and we left it there.

That weekend I had many interesting phone calls with Penny, and I learned so much about Billie. She seemed a lively character, to say the least. Penny told me she would always remember my birthday, think about me at Christmas and get very sad on Mother's Day. She was constantly wondering whether I was happy and whether I would ever get in contact. Penny explained that there was another day she always remembered each year; Billie used to get very emotional around the time of the anniversary of the day she'd had to give me up. I had never thought about that. How very sad. I started to feel guilty that I hadn't thought of her on those days. I wonder whether many adoptees do?

Penny sent me many emails that weekend. Here is an extract from one of them:

> I met Billie when I was just sixteen years old. I was fresh out of school and had taken a job as an apprentice in a local hairdresser's. Billie worked there as a shampooist. From the word go, Billie could only be described as eye catching. She had bright blonde hair, wore full make-up, lots of gold jewellery and colourful clothes. It is really hard to describe her without making her sound like the "brassy barmaid" type; but this was simply not the case with Billie. She was very fussy about her appearance and always wanted to look her best. She absolutely did not want to blend into the background both in

looks or personality. She was a living example of "once seen, never forgotten".

To start with I did not take to Billie at all. To me all women of her age should be like my mother and many other mothers at the time – neutral clothes, shampoo and set hair, sensible shoes. I told my mother that there was a woman at the salon who looked like "mutton dressed as lamb" and immediately dismissed her as such. For her part, Billie seemed very brittle when we first met. She seemed to be quite hardened in her approach, which obviously didn't help, and I could never have foreseen at that point just what a major part she would play in my life.

However, as time passed, and I got to know her, I realised that there was much more to Billie than red lipstick and big earrings. She was much kinder and softer than her initial outward demeanour suggested. She was incredibly funny and interested in other people's stories – with an acid wit that could be totally politically incorrect! But she was the one who could talk to anyone from any walk of life, treating everyone the same, from a tramp sitting in a shop doorway to Lady whoever, who might have come to have her hair done in the salon. This was possibly the most valuable lesson in life I learned from her, and I strive to have the same approach with all those I meet in the way that she did. Billie and I gradually became firm friends, and the greatest bond we discovered we shared was our experience of adoption. She had given up a son for adoption, and I had been adopted. We were opposite sides of the coin and, because of this, we could comfort one another about how it was to be both mother and child in the situation.

Our friendship lasted for thirty years until Billie's death in 2008. During this time I had traced my birth mother, which of course is a story in its own right – so will need to be left for my own book if I ever write it! Billie never forgot "Clive" as she had named him. It had broken her heart to part with him, but she had no choice, like so many other women of that generation. I obviously suggested to Billie that she could try to trace her son, but she was very nervous about doing this. Women in those days were told to go away and get on with their lives – that their babies were going to a "better life" than the one that the birth mother could offer (ridiculous!).

Billie did not want to interfere in her son's life, and I think she hoped that one day he would find her. I pointed out that this might be very difficult for him as she had changed her name (not officially) several times and moved about a lot! Also she had no contact with her family. In all the years I knew her, I only ever met her father, who was very aged and died in the early-1980s. Her sister died when she was young. Her mother had already died, and she had no contact at all with her extended family. How could this poor son have any hope of finding her without a struggle!

As Billie got older and more anxious about life in general, it was clear she would not be able to overcome her fears about seeking out her son. Also I knew from my own experience that mothers doing the tracing have a much tougher time than children, as the law does not support them in the same way. It was clear that Billie no longer had the emotional strength to deal with the upheaval of searching and the roller coaster of emotion that went with it.

Losing Billie was a very difficult time for me as we had always been so close, despite our age difference. We had never been like mother and daughter, despite the perceptions of others that this was the case. However, towards the end of her life, I think Billie did put me in the daughter role, but not in a good way! She hated being immobile and not being able to go out onto the world's stage and "perform". Being old and disabled just wasn't part of Billie's life agenda, and she became very resentful and anxious about everything. She took it out on me because she couldn't with anyone else, but I hated seeing my *dear friend become so cantankerous. This is a very sad period for me to recall and one I would rather not dwell on as we had so many good years together that I prefer to remember.*

Billie died in August 2008. She had a beautiful funeral, just the way she wanted it. Her coffin was white with a gold heart on it, and she had a white hearse. Everyone cried, which again was how she wanted it ("I don't want anyone laughing and joking at my funeral. I want them throwing themselves on the coffin in floods of tears, dear!"), and doves were released outside. Sorting out her possessions was hard. She had very few, and throwing away a person's life is extremely emotional. I found letters she had written to the adoption agency after she had relinquished the baby, which were truly sad to read. I found photos of her with Clive that I had never seen. I kept all of these, telling my husband that I needed to do this in case Clive ever got in touch. I felt so sad because I couldn't imagine how he could ever find me as I wasn't related to Billie, but I hoped one day I might have a chance to put together pieces of the jigsaw for him. I knew how important this would be if he discovered Billie had died before he found her, particularly as I was adopted myself.

In another of her emails, Penny talked about Billie's family:

Her parents were not at all supportive when Billie announced she was pregnant and were more concerned about the neighbours' opinions than Billie's or the child's welfare, which was not uncommon in the socially conservative 1960s. Billie's sister had offered to take the child and bring it up as her own, but in typical theatrical style Billie felt this would be like a re-enactment of the Bette Davis film The Old Maid *and could not bear the thought of having the baby so near and yet so far from her. By all accounts, Billie's parents were pretty cold and distant, particularly her mother. Sadly her sister died when she was in her forties. Billie was very close to her, but as she was living back at home and her brother-in-law did not get on with Billie's parents, it seemed they all got tarred with the same brush and he and her sister's children lost contact. The only contact he ever made with her, when I knew her, was to ring her after her father died to see if the children had been left anything in the will. Billie used to talk about uncles and aunts from her father's side of the family, but I never met anyone. She never spoke of cousins or younger relatives at all.*

So it was all my fault! That's how I felt. Billie had never had any family support or communication from her family for the rest of her life because she'd had me. She had not even received cards on her birthday or at Christmas from any of her family. God, I felt rubbish.

I wanted to meet this woman called Penny, share in her knowledge and love for my blood mother and meet the friends who had attended Billie's funeral. Penny told me she'd had many friends in Brighton, who were very close to her and very fond of her.

I went straight back on the Internet and started to look at accommodation in Brighton, so that I could go there again with my family. I checked my book for gigs. The following week was looking free: my wife and kids were off work and school due to the Easter break. I booked a hotel in Brighton and told Penny I was coming over to see her.

Chapter 9

I was sitting at my desk staring at all the information I'd received over the last few days: pictures, letters, emails, scraps of paper – all filled with stories. It was like looking at a jigsaw puzzle bought from a charity shop with pieces missing.

My conversations with Penny were fascinating. I had never met her or spoken to her before, but I felt so close to her. I had waited so long for answers; she had waited so long for me to get in contact.

I think all adoptees have a natural connection with each other: we have felt similar feelings, have experienced similar lives have and faced the same issues. That weekend, I asked Penny to send me a picture of herself. I really wanted to see what she looked like. After all, she had seen pictures of me as a baby many times over the last thirty years. I knew that, over the last few days, she had seen many pictures of how I looked now. My band has a website, and when I told her I was a jazz musician she had Googled me. She told me she could see a remarkable resemblance to Billie and made comments on my fancy jackets, as she called them. "Billie would have loved seeing all your posh jackets, Steve," she said. "She also wore outrageously loud colourful clothes."

I use a company called Global Stats to monitor my website with their StatCounter tool. It provides information such as number of hits (i.e., people looking at the site), global location of the hits, length of time people spend on the site, most popular pages, music download figures, etc. As I did my weekly check, I was amazed to see the huge number of repetitive hits from Brighton and surrounding areas – and not just from Penny's address. Some views were lasting hours; pictures and music were being downloaded. The StatCounter tool, with the help of Google images, gave me pictures of the houses from where my website was being viewed – many were around Stanwell Street, the area where Billie used to live. Yes, I could see Penny's house, but some were coming from the actual building Billie had lived in. It was interesting to see Billie's flat on Google – the power of the Internet. But who were all these other people?

It was very emotional to look at a screen and see where my blood mother had lived for all these years. I studied the curtains and the flowers in the garden, which she had probably planted. It was a basement flat. I looked at the steps she must have walked up and down hundreds of times.

Seeing pictures of Penny was interesting. She was a pretty girl, the same age as me. Why would she have had a best friend thirty years her age? She had explained, but I thought it was a bit weird. I have friends with the same age gap but these are musician friends. Colleagues I suppose you'd call them – certainly not my best friends.

Penny was also adopted, so we instantly shared the same distinctive experiences. We had grown up in a very different world to other normal people. Only an adoptee would understand the journey. Being adopted is a bit like watching a West End musical where you have walked in late and missed the opening sequence or credit roll, or like watching a TV "who-done-it" mystery where you have missed the murder, or reading a book where the first few pages have been torn out. Talking to Penny about her adoption made me feel as if I wasn't alone in my song with no intro. It made me feel a bit more normal.

In my very early years, I longed to talk to my sister about her feelings on being adopted, but she would never entertain the conversations. My phone conversations with Penny reinforced the fact that we had experienced the same hang-ups and had had the same chips on our shoulders growing up. We seemed quite alike. She would happily talk about her confusion, her feelings of being out-of-place and her lifelong yearning for answers. She had searched for and found her blood mother but didn't say too much about it. I was sure I'd get the full story when we met the following week.

I would be lying if some of the things Penny had said about Billie in her email hadn't hurt me: "She was a brassy barmaid type", "Once seen never forgotten", "She looked like mutton dressed as lamb". Penny had explained those words, putting them into context for me, but it did give me a strange and slightly uncomfortable picture of Billie. Okay, she enjoyed wearing loud clothes, was fussy about her appearance and did not want to blend into the background. She had bright bleached-blonde hair, wore full make up all the time, lots of gold jewellery, bright red lipstick and big earrings. I couldn't help picture her a bit like my adoption rep, Sue – hanging out everywhere. I think I had expected that my blood mother would have dressed in M&S tweed suits, flat brown shoes, long beige skirts and a white blouse, with a scarf in a coordinating colour delicately placed over her shoulders and held in place by an ornate brooch containing precious stones. Billie did sound a little like me, though – not the full make-up, red lipstick and big earrings – but people have said many times to me I am "once seen; never forgotten". I do enjoy wearing loud clothes, and I am a bit fussy about my appearance.

Penny also said Billie had been incredibly funny, always interested in other people's stories, and she'd had an acid wit that could be totally politically incorrect – that also sounds a lot like me. Apparently, Billie was the one who could talk to anyone, from any walk of life, treating everyone the same, from a tramp sitting in a shop doorway to a posh shop client. Yes, that sounds like me too – much to the annoyance of my children.

I found Penny's sense of humour to be similar to mine. We both spoke our minds in a comical, snobby – some might say arrogant – way, to gain attention. I suppose, because Penny had met Billie when she was just sixteen years old, had grown up with her, had been her best friend, had shared a huge part of her life with her and had loved her so much, Billie's character and personality must have had a huge influence on her.

Penny did say the greatest bond they had shared was the experience of adoption. Billie had given me up for adoption, and Penny had been given away for adoption. We were opposite sides of the same coin. So, had it been a mother and daughter relationship? Billie yearning for her child; Penny yearning for her mother. I couldn't wait to find that one out when I visited her in Brighton.

Penny told me on the phone that Billie had thought about me every year on my birthday, without fail, and that the week before and the week after had always been very hard for her. Apparently, Billie got very low around this time each year. I know a lot of adoptees think about their blood mothers on their birthdays, which can be upsetting. Some adoptees enjoy making a big deal out of everyone else's birthday, rather than their own, because they want them to feel special. I've seen it written so many times on the social media: why would anyone want to celebrate the day people were planning to take you away from your mother?

This is a very sensitive subject. After all, birthdays are birth days, the days our mothers gave birth to us, knowing they were going to have to give us up. Many adoptees talk of hating their birthdays, resenting their birth mothers on that day and getting very low, anxious and confused about the separation. Some people prefer to celebrate the day they were adopted rather than their actual birthday. But I can only talk about me; I loved my birthdays in my early years. I was always spoilt with loads of presents. My birthday was for me. It was all about me.

Since the day I'd considered searching for my blood parents – the day my eldest son had been born – I'd thought quite a lot about what had actually happened on the day I was born. I began to feel uncomfortable if, on my birthday, people told me to have a great day, have a happy time, or they told me that they hoped everyone would spoil me on my special day. Special day for whom? Yes, I had been born on that day, but I started to think my separation was being planned on that day. The thoughts of an adoptee are very complex, and I think most of the time we can only partially control them. As another birthday came around, I'd pull my reins in about my recent feelings by thinking how it wasn't really about me; it must have been one hundred times worse for Billie. Also, I still enjoyed getting lots of presents, so decided to make it a special day after all. Mind you, I do enjoy celebrating other people's birthdays more than my own.

I think one way of dealing with being adopted as you are growing up is by thinking about number one – being selfish. That way, you don't allow yourself to think very deeply about things, basically because you're always thinking about yourself and not about others. This does not sound like a very nice coping mechanism, but it is probably one that many adoptees, like me, have used and can relate to. Having children of my own has changed my attitude – it's given me a huge kick up the backside. Doing this research into the adoption process in general and my own adoption in particular has also helped because I am beginning to discover a bit more about who I am and where I came from.

I wondered for years whether I had a half sister or brother – I think because my own sister and I were never really very close. Penny told me that Billie never had or wanted any other children. She had explained to Penny that she'd had one child and it had been taken away, so why would she want anymore? I think that is sad.

Penny talked about how she had encouraged Billie to search for me, but Billie was very nervous about trying. Penny would have known the system as she talked briefly about her search for her blood mother. But, as I had learned from her early letters in the court file, Billie had been told to forget the baby and get on with her own life. The baby was going to have a better life than the one she could provide. Also, it was the law in those days that no contact was to be made with the adopted child. Billie would have signed a court form saying she would have no further contact. I am sure that, had there been a way and Billie had agreed, they both may have tried; Penny would have helped her. But they would have found it near impossible as my surname was never given out to her and the court records containing my parents' names were private. They were very strict about this at the time.

Penny's email said that Billie had hoped I would get in contact one day. That makes me feel very sad. I was just two years too late. But from what I could understand from Penny's email, if I had made contact just before she had died, Billie may have been upset. Why? In her email Penny wrote, "She hated being old, disabled and immobile and was very resentful and anxious about everything. She became very cantankerous." I get the feeling that she may have been extremely angry with me – perhaps aggressive and spiteful. Why? Because I should have been in touch many years earlier, when I could have seen her at her best: quick witted, funny, with her beautiful blonde hair, nice figure, fashionable clothes, bright red lipstick, full make-up and those big bold earrings. I am sure she would not have wanted to meet me for the very first time whilst lying in a hospital bed in Brighton – old, frail, ill, no make-up and fancy earrings, bitter, twisted and confused.

Chapter 10

We started to pack our suitcases and get everything ready for our road trip to Brighton. Anybody with young children will understand how, in situations like this, you end up taking half the house. Although Billie had passed on, I was excited that I was going to meet Penny and fascinated to find out who all those so-called friends of hers were. My family were less enthusiastic, passionate and anxious than me about the trip, but they were looking forward to staying in a nice posh seaside hotel and visiting a place they had never been to before.

The morning we were due to leave, my mother phoned me to tell me that she was very concerned that I was getting in too deep with all this searching. She was extremely insistent that I should think twice about going. She said she feared for my sanity and wondered what I was trying to gain by it. "You've found out who your blood mother was, and she's dead. Why not just leave it like that? Dad and I are very worried about you. Brighton was a place we took you away from, don't you remember? I'll never forget the dark days of your life spent there – have you forgotten? Why are you taking your family there and subjecting them to all of this? Do they know all about this?"

I told her that, yes, they did know and that I probably couldn't do it without them. She said that I was being very silly and selfish, that I was becoming obsessive and hurting Dad and her with all the questions I was asking. She told me I was breaking her heart.

This was the first time Mum had admitted just how this whole thing, this whole searching idea, was affecting the family. She tried so hard to talk me out of going, reminding me of all the special moments we'd shared and the memories we'd built together. She told me that she and Dad loved me so much and didn't understand why I wanted more. She wondered why I was trying to hurt people and break up the family.

I went very quiet on the phone. I now started to question everything about my search.

Yes, I was getting in pretty deep – I knew that. I knew too that I was putting myself right on the line. This obsessive hobby, searching for my inner soul, what the hell was it all about? I was happy as I was, probably the happiest I'd ever been.

I told Mum I had gone this far and had already booked everything; in fact, we were leaving within the hour. She told me I could always change my mind. Once you decide to step on the searching rollercoaster, it is very difficult to get off – not that I wanted to get off. I did want Mum's blessing, but it was very obvious I wasn't going to get it. At the back of my mind, I now felt the guilt of knowing I was hurting my family, the ones who loved and cared for me so much.

All through the journey to Brighton I could hear my mother's words spinning around in my mind. She was right – she was always right. It was affecting me. I was smoking too much and drinking far too much alcohol, and my caffeine intake had become extreme. I could feel my mind go into a place it had never been before. I felt insecure, depressed and slightly insane.

I can completely understand why adoptees wait until their parents pass away before starting a search like this. But the trouble is if you wait too long you're likely to find that your blood parent is too old to enjoy a reunion – or even worse, they are already dead. It's a difficult one.

It was the Easter weekend and the roads were very busy; it seemed as if everyone was driving to their holiday destinations that day. We arrived in Brighton in the late afternoon – and, boy, were we tired! We'd just spent eight long, hot hours in the car. We pulled into the hotel car park feeling absolutely exhausted. Our hotel looked fabulous: a large and extremely elegant

Victorian grade II listed building, overlooking the sea and Brighton pier.

The reception area was amazing. There was a huge Regency-style staircase weaving its way up to the sky, with large mirrors on every wall and crystal chandeliers everywhere. We checked in and our bags were taken to our room. Our art-deco room had a stunning view of the English Channel. We had arrived.

We unpacked, freshened up and decided we would have a walk along the promenade. I had told Penny that I would text her when we arrived. Before we left for our walk, I let Penny know that we had arrived safely and arranged to meet her and her family that night for an evening meal.

It was very strange to be back in Brighton. I had spent many years there, working, walking the streets and playing in bands in seedy, smoke-filled, candle-lit nightclubs. It was all a bit of a haze. I knew Brighton very well, but it had very bad memories for me. It was a place I thought I'd never see again.

We went back to the hotel and dressed for the evening. I had a few large whiskies for courage, and then the four of us made our way down the huge spiral staircase to meet my blood mother's best friend and her family. By now I had started to carry a whisky flask in my back pocket. I never drove under the influence, but having it nearby was becoming a bit of a habit. We had arranged to meet in the hotel reception at 8 o'clock for drinks. The first thing I noticed about Penny was how young she looked. I was taken back; I still couldn't work out why she and Billie had been so close.

We spent over an hour in the hotel bar, talking and drinking wine. They probably thought I was strange; I was being offered glasses of wine but refused them. Instead, I was popping outside to have a cigarette and a large slug of my half bottle of scotch, which I'd stashed inside my jacket pocket.

Penny was a lovely lady. She was humorous, with a huge personality. She was bubbly, sympathetic and extremely well mannered. We got on immediately. The ice had been broken. We did have something in common, though: Billie Parsons.

We all strolled along Brighton promenade, Penny and I arm-in-arm, my wife deep in conversation with Chris, Penny's husband, and the kids playing on the beach in the sunshine. We passed all the places I remembered, such as the famous Grand Hotel, where the rock film Quadrophenia had been filmed, and where, in 1984, the IRA had tried to kill the prime minister, Margaret Thatcher, and her cabinet. We walked along the seafront, where the mods and rockers used to fight.

It was a scorching hot evening. People were still sitting in their deck chairs outside beach huts at 9 o'clock at night, in bikinis and shorts, with "kiss me quick" hats on, reading Mills and Boon paperbacks and eating fish and chips with mushy peas. Finally, we arrived at a small and very quaint Italian restaurant – I think it was a favourite of theirs.

It was a very relaxed and interesting evening. Penny talked to me about her adoption. She told me about how she'd felt growing up – how she had longed for answers. Her story was very different to mine; her blood mother was still alive.

She talked a lot about her birth mother. Penny had eventually managed to trace her with some help from a researcher at the local library, her father-in-law and by searching on the Internet. Unfortunately, she wasn't able to have the reunion she'd hoped for because her blood mother didn't want to know her or meet her. Her open-armed invitation was rejected the day she found out she was looking for her.

Penny had written many letters to her birth mother, hoping she would find it in her heart to meet up. However, it seems that this wasn't a place her blood mother wanted to be in. She had completely disowned her and didn't want to meet her. Unfortunately, this is fairly common when adoptees go in search of their birth mothers.

Penny had persevered. She felt her letters had made no difference. She knew she had to go to her house. So, she went there, knocked on her door and introduced herself. I think I would have done the same. It was a nerve-racking experience as Penny was scared of being rejected again. Her mother had welcomed her in. She had hugged her and told her that she had always known that Penny would come.

At first it seemed as if everything was going to go well from there; however, her mother had not told her other children about Penny. Her mother's husband had known she had given up a child for adoption, but he had made it clear that he did not want to talk about it. The subject had been brought up before, and he didn't want any more said.

Penny did meet her mother again, though – this time with Penny's husband and children. This had meant a great deal to Penny, as she wanted her children to meet their birth grandmother, even if it was only going to be the one time.

This issue of fear remained with Penny's mother. Keeping her secret of having given up a child, and the shame that went with it in those times, had taken its toll. She hadn't told the rest of her family about Penny, and it was a major decision for her to mention it as she risked damaging her relationship with her children. In the end, she decided not to let her children know about Penny. As a result, she has a distant relationship with Penny, which is a shame. I can see it hurts Penny talking about it.

Penny asked me how I was getting on with tracing my father. I told her I hadn't started yet as I had been so overwhelmed with my findings with Billie. I said I would do it when we got back home.

Penny constantly referred to Billie as my mother – your mother did this, your mother did that. I wasn't used to her being called that; whenever I referred to Billie, I always used the term blood mother. I didn't make a fuss about it; I just went with the flow after a while. I actually found it quite nice. I was miles away from my home territory, so I relaxed into it. Mind you, it must have confused my kids, sitting round the table and hearing the conversation. They were great that night. I was very proud of them. They also just went with the flow of the conversation. Enjoying one of their favourite meals helped I think: proper homemade Italian pizza with their favourite toppings.

The wine was flowing and my cigarette breaks were getting more frequent. No one asked me why I wasn't drinking. However, they could probably smell the whisky on my breath. By that time, I could drink quite a lot without it being obvious.

Penny's family were lovely. I discovered that Chris was a teacher at one of the colleges in Brighton. He kept my kids entertained with his funny stories about his teaching days. Although Penny and Chris's kids were older than mine, they spent the evening talking and joking about how to get fake ID and how to get into bars and nightclubs when underage.

Penny told me the story of Billie's funeral. Billie had had many friends in Brighton, and they were all at the funeral. It had been a very emotional service. Billie had stated that she didn't want her funeral to be a happy occasion. Instead, she wanted an emotive and impassioned spectacle. She planned to arrive in a white coffin carried in a white hearse, and, at the sight of this, she imagined people would be hysterical with grief. Then, white doves would be released, as her friends watched on in floods of tears. Apparently, the funeral had gone according to Billie's wishes. There certainly had been plenty of drama. I can totally relate to that, as I want the same. I frequently joke about it to my family and friends – I want a right fuss made. A celebrant had conducted the church service and had read a superb piece about Billie's life, in which I was mentioned.

After the service, her friends had a very lively party to celebrate her life. Many bottles of champagne were consumed, as they talked and laughed for hours about all the happy times they'd had together. Billie had wanted floods of tears at her funeral – which she got – but it was not possible to stop the demonstration of joy and happiness as her friends got together at her wake to celebrate her wonderful, flamboyant life.

I told Penny and Chris about my Brighton years. Chris played a bit of guitar, and he was a big music fan. He was very knowledgeable about the Brighton music scene and knew of the arts magazine I used to run. They had been living in Brighton at the same time as me, so we were able to share our nightclub stories and reminisce about the bands that had been around at that time.

It was very obvious from our conversation that evening that Penny and Chris had been exceptionally close to Billie and knew a great deal about her. They had shared a lot of time together over many years. Just before we ordered our pudding, Penny told me about her plan for the following morning: "We've kept Billie's ashes. They weren't scattered after the Brighton service. Billie had requested that they be kept safe in the hope that her long-lost son would turn up one day. She wanted them to be put in a special place, where her dead partner and lover of many years rested. So, we've arranged another funeral for Billie in Woking, tomorrow morning at ten o'clock. As soon as I knew you were coming over, I contacted all her friends, arranged a service and booked a minister."

So, Penny had announced that the very next morning I was going to be attending my mother's second funeral. I was taken aback, to say the least, but accepted the invitation. We hadn't made any particular plans for the following day. Chris said he would lead the service and leave the religious bit to the minister. He asked me if I wanted to say anything during the service. I didn't know what to say; it was a bit of a shock. In the end, I declined his offer, went outside for a cigarette and downed the last little bit of whisky left in the bottle. I needed to think.

Several months before, I had recorded a cover version of the Everly Brothers' song "All I Have To Do Is Dream". I had a copy of it on CD in the car. I felt the lyrics were appropriate, so I returned to the table and suggested that we play the song at the funeral. Chris thought it was a great idea and said he would supply a CD-player.

For some strange reason, I asked Penny if I could keep half the ashes and take them home with me – take part of Billie back home – so I could put them somewhere I could visit and mark my respects. After all, Woking is a very long way away from where I live. Penny was delighted; she agreed, saying it was a very thoughtful thing to do. I am not sure if this was an alcohol-fuelled idea or a genuine emotionally driven and caring thing to do.

Our first ever evening together ended, and we had all got on extremely well. Penny and I had so much in common; our characters seemed so similar. Why? I think, over the years, she had taken on so many of Billie's characteristics and, genetically, I had a lot of Billie in me – which, of course, sparks off the nature versus nurture debate. Penny made many comments about the similarities between my blood mother and me, such as how I sat, the way I talked and the way I used my hands to express myself. She said she could see so much of Billie in me. I think I may have been wearing one of my fancy jackets that night.

We all walked back to the hotel together before saying our goodbyes and parting for the night. Both sets of kids were running along the still-hot, sandy beach, and the sun was setting over the famous Brighton Marine Palace and Pier. Further along the beach, the remains of the fire-stricken iron structure of the West Pier were being silhouetted by the last little bit of sun. It had been a beautiful, but extremely emotional, evening.

I lay in bed that night wondering how the next morning would be and how the day would pan out. Going to your mother's funeral is hard enough, but going to your blood mother's, whom you've never met, and doing so in the company of all her friends would be strange to say the least. Oh well, my head was already a bit fucked up with all my searching, so a little more poison in the wound wouldn't hurt my anaesthetised soul.

The following morning, after a good breakfast and a head-clearing walk on the beach, I drove with my wife and two boys to Woking crematorium, forty miles outside of Brighton. We arrived just in time for the service. It was a difficult place to find, especially as we didn't know the area. We parked the car and were immediately surrounded by people; we were being introduced to Billie's enthusiastic friends.

My wife and I have been in the theatre/entertainment business for many years and can recognise certain characteristics in people. I looked around me and could tell that, apart from Penny's husband, all of the men at the ceremony were gay – all of them were very beautiful, flamboyant, glamorous homosexuals. It was obvious by their mannerisms, hairstyles, clothes, the way they spoke and the way they carried themselves. So, that was another question I had for Penny and Chris later on. My mother had certainly led a very interesting life, surrounded by wonderful people who had cared for her deeply.

The funeral service was led by the minister of the local parish. We all stood outside in the sunshine, and Chris opened with a few words to reflect on the occasion. As part of this, he said, "We are very pleased and honoured to have Billie's son here today." God knows what my kids were thinking at this stage. Chris went on to say, "Billie used to talk and think about you all the time," at which point all her friends nodded in agreement. I held my wife's hand very tightly; I could feel myself welling up.

The night before, I had decided not to say anything at all; however, standing there amongst Billie's friends, I felt it appropriate to say something. I acknowledged Penny and Chris for arranging the service and everyone for attending. I then went on to thank all the people there for their friendship with Billie and for having cared for her in her final frail years. I concluded by saying how sorry I was that I had been too late in finding her. Then my song was played.

We scattered half the ashes in a particular rose bed, as Billie had requested. The minister read out a prayer, and then we all walked around the garden in a bit of an emotional haze before heading back to the car park.

All the people there were very friendly and seemed so pleased to see me. They commented on how often Billie used to talk about me and how it was great to meet me at last. I had individual chats with all of them, but one conversation stood out and preyed on my mind more that the others. One of Billie's friends specifically wanted to meet me. She took me to one side and said, "Did you know Billie was a spiritualist and a spiritual healer? She may be in contact with you one day. Don't be afraid if she does. She was a very powerful spiritual woman. We were very close friends, and she introduced me to a lot of people on the other side. I'll always be thankful to her for that."

I told her I hadn't realised Billie had been a spiritualist, but that someone at the funeral director's had mentioned something about it. I knew nothing about this subject, so I changed the conversation around by asking her how she had met Billie and about her life and family.

Most of Billie's friends were going back to Brighton, as we were, so I invited all of them back to our hotel for refreshments. I had planned this the night before and had asked the hotel manager to reserve a couple of their best tables for us in a private area of the ballroom, overlooking the sea.

I drove back from Woking emotionally drained. Going to your biological mother's funeral having never had a chance to meet her when she was alive is weird. But I did know a lot about her and did feel a certain amount of affection for her by now. Also, being around people who knew her and loved her and missed her was comforting; that made it very real for me.

The afternoon was a real eye opener; I was formally and informally getting to know Billie's friends and hear their own personal stories of their relationship with her. When I say informally, I mean over many, many bottles of wine!

The previous night, I had spoken with the hotel's catering staff, and we had planned for lots of pots of tea, coffee, cakes and sandwiches to be presented to us on arrival. However, it became clear very early on that the general consensus was that it was time to start drinking wine not tea. I quickly changed my order at the bar, cancelling the tea and coffee and ordering four bottles of their best wine. "No problem, sir. I'll bring them to your table," the waiter replied.

I couldn't believe the size of the wine glasses; they were huge. The four bottles of wine lasted five minutes. I ordered another two bottles, then another, then another. I have never seen so many bottles of wine drunk so quickly in an afternoon. The bottles kept coming; the waiter almost sat down with us.

I decided not to drink that afternoon. I'd never met these people before and wanted to keep a clear head. I'd seen how emotional Billie's friends had been about losing their close friend. I needed to absorb and remember their stories.

It was obvious to me that they thought a lot of Billie. They showed great deal of admiration towards her, and their stories about her demonstrated the love and respect they had for her. They seemed to admire her rude, over-the-top personality, her coarseness, her campness, her glamour and her openness in always speaking her mind. Bits of this I liked; other bits I had reservations about. All of them knew Billie very well and had done so for years. She sounded like a really lively character. I must admit, it also made me feel a little uncomfortable, and perhaps even a little intimidated, as I realised just how well they knew my mother – whereas I didn't. However, they did try to make me feel at ease. They mentioned my website and admitted that they had been on there having a look; they wanted to know what Billie's kid looked like and what he had been up to.

The wine kept flowing and so did the campness. Her gay friends became louder and louder, more flamboyant, more tearful, more emotional talking about their close friend. It was an eye opener to see what Billie's lifestyle in Brighton had been like. I knew Billie had turned to the bottle when she had to give me up. I now wondered whether she had been an alcoholic all her life. I had a quiet word in Penny's ear.

Penny reassured me, "Billie never touched a drop of drink. She liked to have a laugh, but she would never be undignified. In fact, she used to insist on going home if it got a bit over-the-top, especially if there was a lot of drinking going on."

I think Billie must have reached the bottom of the ladder with respect to her drinking once she'd had me and had been admitted to the mental institution. I am glad she decided to stop for good all these years ago.

Chris arrived late at the hotel that afternoon, carrying a large box, which he presented to me. In it was the urn, containing the other half of Billie's ashes, and all of Billie's personal letters, pictures, documents and possessions.

When Chris gave me the box, I immediately felt extremely protective over it. I put it under the table where I was sitting. I felt the things in it were private – between me and Billie – and wanted to look at them by myself, when I was alone. However, someone asked to see some of the photographs, so I opened the box and took out something from the top layer – an envelope containing lots of photographs and a few other things. I then sealed the box back up again.

It now felt almost as if Billie was at the party too. We passed round her pictures, all of which seemed to have long, emotional stories associated with them. Chris was a keen photographer, and there were many pictures of Billie and her friends at parties.

I suppose I must have appeared quite quiet and slightly reserved that afternoon. I certainly wasn't pissed like the others. I decided just to listen to her friends reminiscing. I knew that I could be just as loud and flamboyant as all of them, but I really didn't feel it was the right occasion to compete or show my extravagant side. I was feeling a bit sad; I had just been to a funeral. They were all feeling very happy, getting into the party spirit.

Billie's wedding ring was in the box, together with her crystals, certificates and documents relating to her spiritual healing. There were newspaper cuttings, personal letters and artefacts she had kept and treasured. One of Billie's friends, Duncan, whom I particularly liked, had brought with him the order of service from her original funeral. That was very interesting and told me a lot about Billie. All of the people around me now at the table had been there. Most of them had contributed to the service either by making a speech or writing something about her that was read out during the service.

Billie had been carried into the chapel to Albinoni's *Adagio in G Minor*. The poem "Funeral Blues" – sometimes called "Stop all the clocks" – by W.H. Auden, had been read out. I remember this very moving poem from the film, by the screenwriter Richard Curtis, *Four Weddings and a Funeral*. In the film, the poem was read by Matthew (played by John Hannah) at the funeral of his partner Gareth (played by Simon Callow). "Stop all the clocks, cut off the telephone, prevent the dog from barking with a juicy bone, ..." I love it. I wish I could write like that.

During the service, there had been references to Billie's life in general: where she had lived and the fact that she had not had a happy childhood. Stories, too, about her mother: how she had been a glamorous and very successful concert pianist and how, in later life, she had lost her hearing, become depressed and turned into a spiteful alcoholic and restless soul.

The information contained in the documents and notes from her funeral gave me a wonderful insight into Billie's life:

Billie was an exceptionally vibrant woman, whose life was filled with colour, glitz and glamour. She lived life to the full as a model for beauty magazines. Then, with the outbreak of war, she volunteered as an auxiliary nurse and was posted to Egypt. During this time she contracted and survived meningitis. She rose to the rank of Warrant Officer with the RAF. She experienced the horror of death and terrifying wartime encounters, including rescuing pilots from burning planes.

She fell in love with and then married Teddy. Billie had been looking after a relative of the Queen Mother's in hospital, and, in return for her kindness, she was lent a Bowes-Lyon veil to wear on her wedding day. Teddy came from a very wealthy family, and they lived in a stately home in Northampton, which featured in Homes and Gardens *magazine. Teddy had an affair, which had broken up their marriage because Billie could not forgive him.*

Following the breakup of her marriage, Billie returned to London, to her parents' home, where she did not receive the support she needed. She found comfort in alcohol and had a series of disastrous affairs. During this time of chaos, though, something wonderful did happen: from an affair and a relationship that could not be sustained, Billie had a child, Clive.

They were together for about four months before Clive was adopted. Billie was allowed a minimal amount of contact but, of course, in time that too was lost, and there was nothing left but precious memories and photographs.

There were paragraphs talking about her relationship with Penny and all the healing work she had done at various hospitals in

Brighton, where she cared for patients with terminal illnesses, giving them comfort, counselling and support. She had gained many awards and certificates for her spiritual healing and was part of two miracle cures. (I made a note to myself to ask Penny about these at a later date.) The document from her funeral mentioned that her spirituality had been very important to her. It also talked about her bad language and swearing – and her never-ending flirting. It ended with her friends saying how much they loved her and expressing how much they would miss her.

So I learned a lot more about my blood mother, Billie Parsons, that afternoon. It had been pleasant and very interesting. I did like her friends; they were fun, a bit rude and certainly liked to shock. They obviously loved her wild, extravagant and flamboyant ways; she had probably been very similar to them. They were enjoying having a good time, but I felt it was time to leave them and go back to my room. It was all so much to take in; I needed to absorb things and wind down in a quiet, safe place with my own family. I took my box and explained that I needed to have a rest and would see them later. I had no intention of going back to the party. I felt bad about that, but that's how I wanted it. I imagine the gathering went on for quite a while, although I had overheard someone say that they ought to eat as the alcohol was getting to them.

It was so nice just to sit on my bed and watch the kids play in the room – it was normal, it was safe, it was quiet. I had a quick shower and we left the hotel secretly by the back entrance for a walk along the Brighton promenade again. We walked along the famous historic pier, eating ice creams and enjoying the warmth of the sun on our faces.

There was a colourful little hut on the pier. Beside it was a sign saying "Spiritualist, Psychic, Tarot Cards, Palm Reading and Crystal Ball". All the letters were in different colours. A lady came running out. She shouted, "I must speak to you. I must speak to you now. I've got something to tell you." I was tired, so I politely thanked her and told her perhaps another time. I didn't think anything of it. She was very insistent – she even chased me halfway down the pier – but, at the time, I wasn't in the mood for any fantasy palm reading or spending any money on false dreams about my future.

We left the pier and the mad, multi-coloured lady behind and found a nice place to have our evening meal. It was so good to just sit there and talk about normal things, like choosing what we were going to eat from the menu, and making general chit-chat about nothing in particular.

After our meal we walked through the streets where I used to live. I knew them so well. It felt strange being back in Brighton – especially seeing the houses where I used to spend so much time at wild, psychedelic parties with my old press and band friends all those years ago. I saw the house where one of my friends had died and recognised the street corners where we used to hang out. We walked past nightclubs where I used to play; most of them were boarded up or had changed their names. I didn't tell my family these stories; I was a bit ashamed of my heady days in Brighton.

I still couldn't quite believe I used to live just round the corner from Billie. I must have lived there for two years.

We made our way back to the hotel. All the shops were still open, even though it was very late – it must have been about 10.30pm. Brighton is a cosmopolitan city, very different to our sleepy little village in Devon, where the shops close at 5.30pm on the dot.

After a good night's sleep, we had our breakfast and packed up to leave. I think Penny, Chris and their friends may have wondered where we had got to, as we had vaguely said we would phone them in the morning and perhaps meet up before we left. I just wanted to get on the road, but there was one thing I did want to do before leaving Brighton. I really wanted to see

Billie's flat – the place were she had lived for all these years. I had the address with me; it had been on her death certificate.

We found the address and parked the car nearby. My wife and the kids decided to stay in the car. I got out and noticed a young man putting out the rubbish outside the flat. I went over to him and asked if he lived at this address. He said he did. I explained who I was and that my mother used to live in his house. I must have been convincing as he invited me in.

I was soon walking around in the rooms where Billie had spent so much time. I went into her garden and touched the older, established plants – the ones she had probably planted herself. There was a strange eerie feeling about being in her house. If I were to say I could hear her voice calling my name (Clive), you would think me odd, but I think I did. It was probably nothing. But when I asked the young man whether he ever felt any presence or heard voices or movements in the flat at any time, he told me that he did. He had no explanation for them, but it didn't seem to worry him. His reply was very matter of fact. "You just get used to it. It doesn't bother me. It started when we first moved in."

Suddenly a picture fell off the wall, making me jump. He just carried on with his chores as if nothing had happened, and then he put the picture back on the wall. He explained that he and his girlfriend were happy there and that they had got used to the noises and things moving about. It was a lovely flat, but I had to leave. I thanked the young man for his time, took a picture of the outside of the flat and started my long journey home.

Did I believe what I'd just seen and heard? Did I believe what the chap had to say about it? I don't know. Did I understand what the person in the car park at Woking crematorium had said about Billie being a spiritualist? And what the hell was the old woman on the pier on about? I had to get out of Brighton. It was interesting but fucking weird.

Chapter 11

Coming home from Brighton was emotionally draining, to say the least. Lots of previously unanswered questions were now clear in my mind. We adoptees want to know that our biological parents love us, miss us and think about us, and my visit to Brighton had given me confidence, knowing that Billie had loved me and had thought about me a lot.

It was very sad to have missed Billie by only two years, but, as I said earlier, it may not have been a good experience meeting her two years ago, when she was frail. I should have started my search ten or so years ago. It was comforting to know she had turned her life around. She'd had a good, lively and very happy life, surrounded by a group of close friends, who were great fun to be with and who loved her and really cared about her.

I probably know more about her than I would ever have done if we'd met when she was alive. She wasn't going to tell me about all her dark secrets and difficult times; by the sound of her character, she may have fabricated and exaggerated a lot of the stories anyway.

She never remarried. I think she felt let down by some of the men in her life. I hope I wasn't included in her list. I think that, having given up her baby without any family support and having had a broken marriage and many unsuccessful partners, including Geoff, Billie had become slightly hard and cynical about male sexual relationships.

Penny talked about her being a very beautiful woman, who used to play with men's emotions – flirting with them. She would openly make remarks and comments to good-looking men – more so successful good-looking men; it appears she did admire attractive men who had status.

Penny explained how, in her later years in Brighton, Billie was regularly visited by her GP. She always had to have her hair perfect, be wearing full make-up and be dressed in her best – and loudest – clothes and jewellery. Just for him. She would always pass comment on how handsome he was. "You know, I could kiss you, don't you, Doctor?" she would say. It seems she never opened the door or entertained anybody without wearing her full war paint.

Would Billie have liked me? I think so. I live an interesting life – and have a slightly extravagant and flirtatious lifestyle. Also, I have a very creative and stimulating job in the entertainment industry. I think we are very similar in lots of ways.

My wife also wondered whether Billie would have liked me. But her answer to that was no. I asked why, and she offered a list of reasons: I am a bit old fashioned, very conservative in my dress sense, not one for attracting people's attention by being loud and over the top, I don't drink at all and I don't like loud, crowded parties. She didn't think Billie would have liked me at all.

I gave myself a day or so to recover from Brighton, and then I decided to have a look in the box Chris had given me. We'd had a quick look inside on the day of the funeral, but there were still lots of things in there I hadn't seen.

I pulled out a black bag, which was sealed with lots of Sellotape. Very carefully, I started to remove the tape. I opened the bag and pulled out an old, scruffy cuddly toy. Then I realised it was a panda – but not any old panda; it looked like the one Billie had given to the adoption agency, which was then sent on to my parents. This was the panda that I'd received on my first Christmas. Mum used to tell me it had come from someone very special. I now know it was a present from Billie because she mentioned it in one of the letters in my court file. I treasured that toy panda. How did she get it? How did she get it back? Surely, it couldn't be the same one.

When I lived in Brighton I used to sell things at the church jumble sales for extra money. I remember going home to my parents' house, climbing up into the loft and collecting some of my old toys so that I could sell them – my old Tri-ang and Hornby train sets, my Dinky and Corgi cars, my Batman books and my James Bond guns and toys. I also remember that one of my trips to the loft had involved getting rid of my old panda.

I thought about those table-top sales. I didn't always go to them myself; I had a friend who sometimes did them for me. He knew more than me about collectable items and memorabilia. He would take a cut, but he always got a good price for things.

I have a vague recollection of him telling me that a lady had bought the panda and that she had asked a lot of questions about it, such as where it had come from. She bought only the panda; she hadn't been interested in anything else.

It certainly looked like mine. Had she really gone to the sale that day in Brighton and seen the soft toy she had given me all those years ago? I now had it back. Was it really the panda she had given me or was it something very similar? It does look very much like it – very old and scruffy, just as I remember it in its later years. I couldn't be sure. I carefully put it back in its bag.

If it were the panda, and I had been the one at that table-top sale that day, and a woman had come up to me and asked questions about the panda, told me why she wanted it and explained who she was, my life would be so different today. That would have been an opportunity for me to meet my blood mother.

In the box, along with all the pictures, documents and artefacts, was the urn, which contained Billie's ashes. I was okay about it. In fact, there was something quite nice about bringing it back to where I lived. Some of my friends thought it was strange that I wanted to have her ashes in my house. I was very much okay about it. I think some people do keep a small amount of a loved one's ashes as a keepsake.

I put the urn, still in its bag, under my piano next to my office/studio. Quite often, when I was alone, I found myself talking to the urn. Was I going mad? I mentioned this to other people, who had also kept a relative's ashes, and it seemed a normal thing to do. So, I was also okay about talking to it – that is, until things started to happen around the house. Inexplicable things.

Occasionally, the lights would flicker on and off. Sometimes, in the evening, the whole house would go into darkness for no reason. This was something my electrician could not explain – after I'd got him out a few times to inspect the electrics. Things started falling out of cupboards when nobody was anywhere near them. The tap would suddenly turn itself on, and the water would flow. Also, when I was alone in the house, I could smell a strange perfume and sometimes feel someone touching my skin and head. I started seeing shadows out of the corner of my eye.

My music producer – who is also a good friend of mine – came round one afternoon. We had planned to check an arrangement of a song I had written. A couple of days before, I had carefully arranged all the controls on my mixing desk – volume levels, effect patterns, treble and bass settings. A mixing desk has many switches and controllable knobs on it. That day, when we sat down to look at the song, everything had been changed on my desk. All the controls had been moved to point in a certain direction.

My friend, Colin, who knew my story, had a brother who was a regular visitor to mediums and spiritualist churches. He knew a lot about the subject, and he immediately showed me where all my controls were pointing to: the urn underneath the piano.

I told him about things moving and the other incidents around the house, and he explained that it sometimes happened in his house too. He continued, "Don't be afraid of them. Cherish them as it takes them a lot of energy to do these things." I listened to his story. His uncle, who had died years ago, was in communication with him and his brother. He said this was a common occurrence when someone wanted to let you know they were around and were thinking of you. He told me that, if I was upset, uncomfortable or uneasy about any of the things that were happening, I'd just to tell them politely to stop it. I thought it all sounded a little crazy and told him so.

I don't know why, but I was not frightened at all by the happenings in the house, and neither were the other members of my family, for some reason. Things had been moving around inexplicably – not flying around the room as such, but they would be in a different place to where they had been left. There were constant electrical malfunctions, strange shadow movements and things had fallen off shelves. We all just used to laugh at it and say, "Oops, that's Billie at it again!"

There are a couple of very nice old ladies who come to my jazz concerts regularly. I knew that they were very interested in tracing family trees and, whenever I saw them at gigs, I kept them up-to-date on how I was getting on with my search for my parents and, more recently, about the strange happenings around the house. They just looked at me and smiled.

They were regular visitors to a nearby spiritualist church. They were familiar with happenings like this and had experienced similar things themselves. "They do like to play around with electricity, my dear," the first relied. "Do you occasionally see unexplained shadows in the house?" asked the second. Well, yes, I had – ever since I'd brought the urn back from Brighton. This was all getting a little bit spooky.

My two lovely old ladies, Connie and Stella, invited me to attend a session at their church. I said I would think about it. I do not belief in the afterlife, nor do I believe in spirits. I do have a very open mind, though. I was intrigued by their knowledge on the subject and about the goings-on in the house, but I really didn't want to explore it any further.

The phone rang at home. It was Stella, saying that she had made me an appointment to see someone at their church. It was in a month's time. I had no reason to decline; I knew I had plenty of time to think of a reason not to go and then politely cancel it.

Weeks went by, and I forgot all about it until a couple of days before the appointment, when Stella phoned to remind me. She said she was also going that day, so she would meet me at the church. I agree to see her there; however, I was quietly cursing myself for having forgotten to cancel.

I purposely didn't tell anyone of my intentions to visit a medium or a spiritualist church as it all seemed a bit far-fetched and a little strange and unknown. My wife knew, of course, but warned me against it. However, she knew me very well and had seen my reaction to the results of my search. I had an open mind to most things – some would say too open – and she knew that. Also, when I get something in my head, I tend to just go for it. I certainly didn't tell my mum and dad I was going; they would have thought I had completely lost my senses.

The day came. I jumped into the car and turned up at the church early. It was not a traditional church – more of a modern church-hall type of building. The reception looked like a library with hundreds of books about the subject of spiritualism on shelves around the walls. I was greeted by the lady who ran the organisation. She checked whether I had an appointment and offered me a cup of tea. I sat down at a large wooden table with other people who were waiting for their appointments.

It was very obvious that they all believed in this phenomenon and were regular visitors to the church. I was polite and curious. I knew nothing about the subject and really had no belief at all, but I was open to their ideas and welcomed their thoughts, listened to their stories and respected their feelings and faith – if you can call it that. They seemed perfectly normal. None of them appeared to be strange in any way. Most of the people there went every week or month for comfort and communication with their loved ones who had passed away. They told me many stories of events that had happened to them. I just smiled and listened.

I began to smell the perfume again and asked if anyone else could smell something. They said they couldn't. They did ask what kind of smell, and I said I sometimes smell a strange perfume. One of the ladies laughed and said, "You could be in for an interesting afternoon, dear." She started to relay a story to me about her late husband who was obsessed by a certain type of soap. She hated it and used to hide it. She would buy a different brand for him, but he always found the old one. She laughed again and said, "I can still smell his soap around the house."

One of the ladies was fiddling with, what looked like, an egg timer. I just had to ask her what it was for. She replied, "The lady upstairs sometimes gets carried away in the other world, and she has to be called back in time for her next appointment as we are all given just half-an-hour."

Fucking hell, what other world? Jesus Christ, what was I getting into? Of course, I didn't say that to the ladies – but I thought it.

All of the people attending that day were very happy and contented and received comfort of some kind by visiting the church. All had relatives or loved ones who had passed away, and it seemed that their regular visits offered them a satisfaction through their communication with those they had lost. I was the youngest one there – and the most sceptical – but I was in their building, their church, drinking their tea, so I listened and politely respected their time and space and awaited my appointment.

Their belief in the system appeared a bit nutty, but they didn't seem mad or strange in any way at all – normal people, just waiting their turn, like in a doctor's surgery. I felt as if they were all waiting at a train station for friends they hadn't seen for a long time to turn up. They knew they were on the train, and they were just waiting for it to stop and for them to get out and stand on the platform.

They told me this lady was good – one of the best. *One of the best at what*, I thought. They went on to say, "We get a lot of mediums who visit our church. This lady comes once a year. She costs a lot of money, but she's amazing; she's so in touch with the other side." *The other side of what*, I thought. Then the egg-timer lady said, "Your turn. First door on the left at the top of the stairs." I could hear the thirty clicks on the egg timer turn to thirty minutes as I walked up the stairway to heaven.

I knocked nervously on the door and was greeted by a small, pleasant-looking lady with long blonde hair. I was surprised; she was younger than I had imagined and she was wearing normal clothes. Had I watched too many films, walked on too many seaside piers or visited too many fairgrounds? I had obviously seen too many extravagant fortune tellers, wearing bright turbans over their long jet-black hair, displaying lavish jewels, dressed in brightly coloured clothes and clutching a large glass ball with long, painted fingernails.

No, she just looked normal: a petite, busty lady in a plain skirt, blouse and jacket, with long black boots.

Upstairs was a meeting room of some kind. Seats were arranged in a semi-circle, with a podium in the middle and pictures of Jesus Christ on the walls. There was a table and two chairs in one corner of the room.

She walked to her chair and sat down and invited me to sit opposite her. She asked if she could hold my hand for a moment. She asked my name then quietly introduced herself. (I have chosen not to disclose her name.) She also asked whether I had ever seen a medium before. I told her I hadn't.

There was a small table between us. On the table, there was a glass, a jug of water and a box of tissues. I couldn't work out what the tissues were for at all.

She sat back in her chair and explained she would be going in and out of what may appear to be a sleepy state of consciousness. She told me not to worry or be nervous. She closed her eyes for a few seconds, lifted her head back, clasped her hands and said, "Someone is coming through. Someone is with us who wants to talk to you."

I started to smell that perfume again – the same one that the letters smelt of in my court file, only stronger.

I asked the medium if she could smell perfume. She said, "Yes, I can. It's old ... it's an old fragrance." She appeared to be trying to calm someone down and, in a raised voice, told the person to wait. Then she said, "We have a lady with us today who wants to speak to you. She is very persistent." Then, in a loud voice, she continued, "Stop swearing! Stop shouting at me! Just wait a minute." To me, she said, "God, this woman has strong powers. She is saying you are her child, her son. Does this mean anything to you? Is she your mother?"

I explained that it was a long story but that, yes, she could be. She kept asking her to calm down and stop shouting. I knew Billie was loud and brash; it did sound as if this could be Billie, but I didn't say anything.

The lady asked me if there was anything I wanted to say to her. Cynically, I asked, "Could you please tell me her name?" She hesitated and replied, "They don't usually tell me their names, dear, but wait ... wait." She gave a loud sigh, opened her eyes fully, then closed them again tightly and said, "Billie." She then continued, "Billie's a unique lady. I've never come across anyone like her before."

That was enough to let me know something very real was happening here.

I said quietly, "I think she is my blood mother. I was adopted."

"That is who she says she is. I just wanted to check with you. Do you want to ask her anything?" she replied.

"I just want to thank her for having me and for letting me go ... and I want to let her know I had a great childhood with very loving parents ... and I was okay. Please tell her I'm sorry for contacting her so late in my life and sorry for hurting her. Could you also tell her I've met her close friend Penny."

"She says she knows, dear. Keep in contact with her, Clive, and pass on my love ... and say sorry to her for being very bad tempered with her before I passed over."

Billie went on to tell me, through the medium, that she was happy that I had her ashes and that I was never to put them anywhere, especially my garden as I was going to move. She wanted me to keep them with me. She said she was very proud of me and proud of what I had achieved so far in my life. She also mentioned she liked my music and my fancy jackets.

I then realised why there was a box of tissues on the table. I took a handful and wiped away my tears.

Suddenly, there was a knock on the door; it was the lady with the egg timer. My time was up.

I thanked the medium and gave her a kiss on the cheek. She just smiled, fiddled with her hair and said, "I hope I've helped. God, that woman is strong. I've never had anyone that powerful come through before." I replied, "Yes, you've helped. Thank you."

I came back downstairs, holding the stair rail tightly with one hand and clutching my handful of tissues in the other. One person from the group stood up and handed me a piece of paper and a pen saying, "You must write all the things down – all the details she told you. You don't want to forget them. Do it now."

"Don't worry," I said politely, "I won't forget them."

One member of the group offered me another cup of tea but I declined; it was certainly one of those moments where I just wanted to be by myself. I paid the secretary of the church and, slightly dazed and confused by the experience, I left the building and headed back into a cold, bustling high street.

As I walked back to my car, I looked around at the faces of the passers-by and wondered whether they knew where I'd been. I had a feeling that they did. I felt a bit like a naughty schoolboy who had just stolen something and got caught. Did I look any different? Could they tell what I had just experienced? Was there anything around me that they could see and I couldn't? I felt very out of place being with other people.

Driving home I heard repeatedly in my head the words the medium had said. How did she know Billie's name? It was something I had not mentioned to anybody apart from my very close family and friends. How did she know about the ashes? How did she know I had them and was thinking of putting them in my garden? How did she know about my music and my fancy jackets? How did she know my name had been Clive? Stella and Connie, who recommended the church to me, knew a bit about my searching, but they certainly didn't know my blood mother's name, or my birth name, or that I was considering putting Billie's ashes in my garden.

That evening I phoned Stella and Connie and asked them to be honest with me about whether they had told the medium anything about my searching or anything at all about me. They assured me they had not and that they, too, had had an interesting afternoon.

I have known my little old ladies for a very long time; I believed them. There was no reason at all why they would feed information across to try to upset me or confuse me, convert me or try to paint over my already-colourful canvas. Also, Stella and Connie didn't know half of the information the medium had given me. They went on to say that the spiritual world is a remarkable place, and that they believed in it without any doubt. Connie is also a spiritual healer and, at gigs, is constantly telling me that she can feel the spirits around her. I think she is funny – a bit cranky, but funny. Stella usually drives her to my gigs and, during the interval, she quite often talks openly about people who have died on the road she has just travelled on. I remember playing at one particular gig at a golf club, and Connie had refused to sit on the only seat left in the room. She made a big fuss about it; she said someone had died in the chair and was still sitting in it. That made me laugh at the time.

My experience at the church sounds a bit crazy. I hadn't prepared any questions before I met the medium. I really didn't think anything would happen. Afterwards, I could think of lots of things that I should have asked.

So do I believe in mediums, spiritualism and spiritual churches? I would say not. Would I go back? Probably not either. Would I recommend the experience to others? I don't think so, but I don't know. So why did I do it? Well, as my blood mother had been a spiritualist, going to a spiritualist church to talk to her was the logical thing to do.

I put the day's experience down as being just another strange and inquisitive part of my mixed-up search. If it were true, then I had done what most adopted people want to do: I had thanked my blood mother for the adoption. I had spoken to Billie and thanked her for having me and for releasing me for adoption. I had let her know that I had turned out okay and that I'd had a great upbringing with superb and very loving parents.

I remembered the women on Brighton pier – the psychic, tarot, palm-reading, crystal-ball lady. She had been so insistent about talking to me that afternoon; she chased me half way down the pier. Was that Billie wanting to talk to me? Then there was the lady at Arka funeral directors, who had told me how strange it had felt in the office on the day of Billie's funeral. And finally, at Woking crematorium, the person had told me that Billie might get in contact one day. Who knows? It all sounds a bit crazy to me.

Chapter 12

My afternoon at the church was one of the strangest moments in my life. Had it been real? Had I really been talking to Billie?

I came to the conclusion that I wasn't sure. I decided that, if anyone were to ask me about it, I'd have to put it down to the fact that some mediums are very clever and that it was all part of my research. After all, I didn't want to appear weird.

I did want to talk about it, though. When I got home, my wife listened to my account of what had happened. She told me she didn't believe in those kinds of things but, if I was happy holding those thoughts and it was part of my healing and answered my questions, then that was the main thing. So we just left it like that. I certainly didn't tell my kids.

My story of that afternoon wasn't going to make sense to many people. However, I decided to meet with my record producer again; he knew about these things and believed in communicating with spirits through mediums. He was fascinated by my story; he believed every word. He said that he never mentions his experiences to anyone – well, apart from his brother. He told me to be careful about telling people as there is no concrete proof that any of this kind of thing exists. He didn't want me to make a fool of myself. His advice was that I ought to keep it to myself. I think he was trying to preserve my sanity in the eyes of the public.

A huge weight was off my shoulders, though. Most adoptees want to try to make contact with their blood mothers – to thank them, I suppose. And from their side, blood mothers want to know they are thought about, too. I genuinely think I did both of these things. Billie had been a spiritualist, so I had gone to find her in a spiritualist church.

I felt it was time to contact Sue again, my adoption rep. I had missed her during all of this. I'd been through so much since our last meeting, and I wanted to catch up and tell her about my findings. The last time Sue and I met was when I'd received the letter from NORCAP telling me Billie had died. I had then shot off at a tangent on my own and contacted Penny. I phoned Sue's office to make another appointment.

It was nice to see her again. She listened to my latest stories. She seemed amazed at my persistence and admired my tolerance – and was a bit freaked out by my spiritual experience. She was fascinated by it, though. Then I mentioned that Billie was with us. "She's under the piano, you know." We both looked at each other, her eyes staring in shock and her mouth wide open. "I'm only joking, Sue," I said. But I wasn't. I decided it was best not to mention the strange movements and happenings that had been taking place in the house recently. Just as I told her that I was joking, the kitchen tap started to run and the lights flickered. I calmly walked through and turned off the tap – and said nothing.

Sue turned the conversation to my blood father, asking me what information we had to go on. I had his name (Boyce), occupation, age and address at the time of my adoption. He was also going to be relatively old by now.

I mentioned Facebook, but Sue wasn't a big fan of Facebook. She said it was an extremely dangerous way to search for people. She explained that it was quite a new thing, and more and more people were using it as a way of tracing adopted family members. She said one of the drawbacks was it was so quick, so immediate – too quick, too immediate, in fact. People can be unprepared on both sides. Also, many people are very unhappy and shocked when approached this way. She was concerned it was too public and may cause family members a lot of hurt emotionally. She was also worried that people who use Facebook are usually alone when doing so – whether alone in their room or alone in their head. Either way, they are unsupervised or unsupported when using it.

I agree with her, so I quickly made a note of a few technical points for people who are thinking about searching, or for people who have had children adopted and want to keep it private. Here are the points I made: make sure only friends can see your profile; think carefully about whom you accept as friends, make sure you can only receive messages from your friends; review who can post on your wall; make sure your contact details are not on your profile page. All these things can be controlled in your account settings and privacy settings.

Sue went on to say that some people can get very excited – too excited – and don't stop to think about the impact they are going to have on the person they have just found. She relayed a story about one of her clients who found her blood mother on Facebook. She had sent a message but, as she hadn't heard back, she had presumed her mother didn't want to have a reunion and didn't care about her. It turned out that, although her mother was on Facebook, she didn't really use it; in fact, she never looked at it. Believing she'd been rejected by her mother again, Sue's client became depressed and eventually committed suicide.

Sue really made a point about being guided and helped through a reunion process. The law in the UK is, if you were adopted before 12 November 1975, as I was, and don't know your birth name, you need to apply to the Registrar General for your original birth certificate. Also, you have to receive counselling, and they make arrangements for you to meet with an adoption adviser – mine, of course, was Sue. If you were adopted after that date, you are basically on your own, which I think is a big worry and concern. I strongly agree with Sue, my councillor and adviser, that it is very useful on all accounts. I do worry about people just diving into this deep emotional ocean with no guidance.

Sue and I sat down at my computer and started to put the name Boyce into her designated websites. It's quite a common name; this was going to take some time. We tried the death register but had no joy there. Sue had a new contact on that front, so it was really up-to-date – unlike our experience with our search for Billie. But there was nothing there, which meant that he might still be alive – well into his eighties, but still alive! I know some very fit eighty-year-olds. We were potentially onto something.

I was going to try all angles, so I decided I would write to the address I had in my adoption file: the home address of the Boyce family, an address where he'd lived over forty years ago. It was a complete long shot, but some people do stay in the same house for years, or else they pass it on to family members. Also, many people still remember the person they bought their house from and may have an up-to-date contact address. I occasionally get the odd letter for a previous occupant who lived in my house over twenty years ago.

I worded the letter carefully, as if I were seeking a family contact who used to live at that address – nothing personal or obtrusive, just a brief, friendly note. I also enclosed a stamped addressed envelope.

A week or so later I received a kind letter from the lady currently living at that address. She explained that she did not know of anyone called Boyce; however, she knew of an old lady who had lived in the street all her life, who might remember the family. She was planning to speak to the old lady to find out if the name was familiar to her or whether she could remember anything about the previous residents. And sure enough, she did look into it for me. She wrote back, explaining that she had spoken to the old lady and had passed my letter onto her. I replied to thank her for her kindness and sent her some flowers to show my appreciation.

I then received a letter from the old lady. In it she wrote: "There was a couple living in the house many years ago called Boyce. They moved to Ottershaw, in Surrey, but they had always talked about emigrating to Australia. There was a brother, I think, who lived nearby. He had two daughters who died in their early teens. I can't remember much more than that, sorry. Not a lot of help, unfortunately, but it's the best I can do. Regards, Grace."

But it was helpful; it gave me a new angle. Australia – I couldn't think of anywhere further away. This wasn't going to be easy! I also sent Grace some flowers and wrote her a letter to thank her for her time and let her know that her information had been very helpful.

This was going to be difficult, if not impossible. I was not sure what to do to follow up on this lead. Australia is over ten thousand miles away from England. Was I going to drop everything and fly out there? It would be an expensive trip to fly to the opposite side of the world for a possible meeting and a cup of tea with my old dad – who may or may not want to see me. I decided at the time I probably would if I had to.

I thought about trying NORCAP again. I'd had success with them when looking for Billie. I'd got results quickly and I felt that, with them, my money had been well spent. If my search was going to be in Australia, I would need their contacts. I rang them, but there was no answer. I tried again an hour later – still no answer.

I filled in all their forms and prepared a cheque. I just wanted to check whether the amount was correct before sending it off. My involvement with them when I was looking for Billie was limited. They had searched and had found her death certificate. They had simply informed me that Billie had already died, so there was no further research for them to do. If Geoff was still alive, and living in Australia, it was going to cost me more than their normal fee. I wanted to talk to someone about it. I kept phoning but, still, I was getting no answer.

The following morning I tried again. This time the phone line was dead. I tried to find their website. I put the name into Google and their site came up. At the top of the page was a short paragraph explaining that AAA-NORCAP had gone into administration. Apparently, they had ceased trading, and their register was no longer active.

I checked with some of the adoption social networks. They were going crazy with people wanting to know more information – people who were halfway through their searches, people who had paid quite a lot of money, hoping they would find results. And now, these people were finding that their offices had been closed.

I'm not sure why it had come about or how it all ended up. NORCAP was a charity organisation; I think they basically ran out of funds. I didn't post my envelope that day.

Sue came round again, and we both went back to the Internet to continue the search. We looked at the UK telephone directory; there were hundreds of Boyces listed. We tried to focus in on the area where they used to live. We sat at my computer, printing off names and telephone numbers of potential Boyces living around that area. People do move, but we knew that some people move only within a fifty-mile radius of where they used to live. We were hoping to find family members living within that radius who would know the whereabouts of Geoff.

Sue told me it was time to make some phone calls. She asked if I wanted her to do it, but I was quite happy to make the calls. She asked me what I was going to say. I don't mind a bit of acting or role-play, so I gave her my ad-lib script. In my posh, caring voice, I began, "Good afternoon. Sorry to trouble you, but I am trying to trace a member of my family. The name is Geoff Boyce. He is in his eighties. I wonder if you could help me?"

I had done a lot of telephone sales in my day, and I think I persuaded Sue that I would not go in like a bull in a china shop or start to be over-persuasive, insensitive or aggressive. After my little role-play with her, she gave me the okay to make the first real call.

I dialled the first number on my long list, desperately hoping that I would stumble upon someone who would know Geoff

Boyce. We spent all afternoon on the phone. Sue stayed with me; as she wanted to ensure that my wording was right and that I was coming across in an appropriate manner. I made sure I was being diplomatic and sympathetic in my approach.

I spent hours on the phone, saying the same thing over and over again. Sue was busy on her laptop, working on some other avenues of research. The time passed quickly. It was getting late, and I'd come up with nothing. Sue looked at her watch and said she had to leave, so we said our goodbyes. I was left staring at a piece of paper with a list of names and telephone numbers on it. I had crossed off in red pen the ones I had already tried; there were still another ten to do.

When working in telesales or call centres it is important not to get upset by the number of negative calls you make. Your voice always has to remain enthusiastic and positive. You end up drinking lots of coffee and smoking lots of cigarettes. But you carry on; you just keep phoning. I had no target or call rate, but what I did have was a huge incentive: I wanted to find my blood father. That was bigger than any financial incentive or commission prize.

I sat back down at my desk and decided to keep phoning – call after call, saying the same thing, hoping to hit my target. Then, at around 5 o'clock, I heard the words I had been longing to hear. The second-last call on my list was a hit. I had sold the front page.

A lady answered the phone. I said my script: "Good afternoon. Sorry to trouble you, but I am trying to trace a member of my family. The name is Geoff Boyce. He is in his eighties. I wonder if you could help me?"

The lady replied, "Yes, he was my father's brother. Unfortunately, he died nearly thirty years ago."

I had to make sure she was talking about the right person. I repeated the name, and then I gave her more of the details I had about Geoff: his occupation, address and date of birth. I mentioned that he'd had a daughter who had died at a very early age. I hoped we were not talking about the same man. I needed to make sure.

She replied, "Yes, I do know who you're talking about." She wanted to know why I was calling. She was a bit defensive about offering any additional information, which was understandable. She clearly knew of the man I was looking for. She asked who I was.

I was in a bit of an emotional state, having just heard for the first time that my blood father had passed away. Through my tears, I very softly explained my situation. "I am his son." She snapped back at me, "But you can't be; Geoff didn't have a son."

She did not believe me and went on to say that Geoff's wife was still alive and living in England. "She knows nothing of this," she maintained. The lady insisted that I give her my telephone number. I suppose I could have hung up; I had the information I was looking for. But I knew she would be able to get my number using the call-back system, so I gave it to her. She was obviously annoyed by my phone call. She repeated, "Geoff never had a son. I think you're making all of this up." I could tell she thought I was a hoax caller by her next words: "What are you looking for?" I replied that I was just trying to trace my blood father, as I'd been adopted. She put the phone down abruptly, without saying goodbye.

I sat and stared at the phone and cried. I went into the kitchen, opened the cupboard, reached for an unopened bottle of whisky, unscrewed the cap and took a big slug straight out of the bottle.

A few hours later, the phone rang. My wife answered it and passed the receiver over to me. It was Geoff's wife. Fuck, this was going to be the most difficult phone call I was ever going to take. I walked upstairs to be alone.

I asked her if we were talking about the right person. I gave her the information I had: his full name, address, date of birth, occupation, colour of hair, salary at the time and the details about his three-and-a-half-year-old daughter. "Are we talking about the same man?" I asked.

There was a silence on the end of the phone. I knew so much about Geoff – well, enough to convince her I was someone important. Even to this day, I still clearly remember saying the words to her: "He was my father." We both cried. She knew nothing about me at all. Geoff had kept me a secret.

I went on, very softly and gently, to explain how, in 1961, he'd had an affair with a lady, and they'd had a child: me. She kept saying that it couldn't be, but I felt that she knew it to be the truth. She told me that, around the time their daughter died, their relationship had been stretched by the grief they'd experienced at the loss of their little girl. Geoff had taken it particularly badly and had spent a lot of time away.

She wasn't angry at all. In a sympathetic voice she said, "This is not your fault. It's not your fault, you know."

I told her I had lots of paperwork, including the adoption court files, which backed up the story. She asked me how it could have happened, and I explained that my blood mother and Geoff had met at a hospital ball, somewhere in London. This seemed to make some kind of sense to her as she then said, "Yes, he did go away a lot after our daughter passed away." I think she realised that I knew too much information for her to question my statements; she started to believe me.

She went on to explain how, shortly after their daughter died, they had moved to Australia as Geoff had had great job prospects out there. When he died, at age fifty-eight, she had sold their beautiful apartment by the sea and moved back to England.

One of the things she repeatedly said was that, if he had told her at the time, they would have adopted me. They were not able to have any more children after their daughter died of cystic fibrosis. She said, "Geoff and I could have looked after you and cared for you." It was a very emotional phone call for both of us.

We ended the call – both of us in tears – agreeing that we both needed time to think and that we would talk again.

I put the phone down, still in tears. I had just done what I had never wanted to do: I'd hurt someone in my search – really hurt someone. It was something my mother had warned me about. It was also something Sue, my adoption rep, had told me might happen, right at the very beginning of my search. Geoff's wife had had no idea he'd had a child. He had never told her or any of his family, by the sounds of it. She must now be thinking that Geoff – her long-lost, loving husband – was a liar and a cheat and had kept the biggest secret anyone could have kept from a wife: he'd had a son by another woman.

It hurt me to learn that Geoff had never told his wife or family about me. I suppose, at the time, Geoff was being asked to cut off his emotional ties with his baby – just like Billie was. However, because Geoff never told anyone about me, I will never know if he ever thought about me at all.

After putting the receiver down, I went through so many emotions. I was so sad to hear he had died – he had only been fifty-eight. But I also felt guilty that I had revealed my story to Geoff's wife. She had repeatedly told me that it was not my fault, but it felt as if it was. I felt terrible.

My wife knew of my conversation that day; she had been listening at the bedroom door to our phone call. I was okay about that. She was there to give me a big hug afterwards.

By this time, my kids were shouting at me to come downstairs and make their supper. After a quick cigarette and another large scotch, I went back to the daily dad grind.

What an emotional week I'd just had! I had started my search in hope of, one day, meeting Billie and Geoff. Now, finding out they were both dead was a massive shock. I still needed to have more information about Geoff, though. I want to know more about his life. I wondered whether he had ever mentioned me to anyone.

Chapter 13

Discovering Geoff had died was very sad, but I was determined to find out more about the man and why he couldn't stay with Billie, or look after Billie and me from a distance.

Did he move to Australia because Billie was becoming too emotionally reliant on him? Did he move to the furthest part of the world because he couldn't handle his emotions having fathered a child whom he could never see, but who would be growing up in the same country as him? Was he running away from his responsibilities, or avoiding the shame he would feel, should his family ever find out?

He and his wife could start a whole new life in Australia – a fresh new life. He could forget anything had ever happened. When Billie was drinking heavily and spending time in the mental institution, having had me, Geoff may have found it all too much. I knew that Billie could be a larger-than-life character; no doubt, her outgoing and demanding nature would have been extremely emotionally draining on him. I wanted answers.

Billie had been so insistent about me having a father figure in my life. She wanted a strong male influence in my upbringing. Perhaps she felt that her father had not loved her enough. Penny talked about Billie's parents being very cold and distant with her, even at an early age. Or perhaps she simply understood how important it is for a boy to have a father around.

I was still looking at unmarried girls pushing prams in the street – still looking at their fingers for wedding rings. I didn't feel angry anymore. I had actually started to feel sorry for them – well, sorry for the babies because they may not have had a father around. Why are there so many of them?

I remembered the government's figures from the ONS, which stated that there are approximately two million lone parents with dependent children in the UK, and that women account for ninety-one per cent of these lone parents. I found further information from a company called Gingerbread (a charity for UK single parent families). They agreed with the ONS's figures and also explained that forty-one per cent of children in single-parent families live in relative poverty. Gingerbread reiterated the government's figures that only nine per cent of single parents are men. Apparently the proportion of lone parents who are men has remained at this level for over a decade. So, there are over three million children living in single parent families, most of them without fathers.

Where do all the fathers go? Why are the dads not around to help bring up their children? And why are there so many single parents these days? Apparently, one in four children does not have an active, present father. I was shocked by that figure.

Some couples do try for many years to work things out and decide eventually to get divorced. It is probably not good for children to be in an environment where the parents are arguing all the time because they do not love each other anymore.

I do not know the answers, but I do know a baby does put an enormous amount of pressure on a relationship. It changes the relationship enormously.

Take this scenario: you fall in love with a beautiful girl, who always dresses in a feminine way. She looks after her body, goes to fitness classes, visits her hair salon every two weeks and always smells of expensive perfume. She is intelligent and has many interests and friends. You both have an active social life. You go to parties, restaurants and the theatre. You go for long romantic drives in the country, occasionally staying in posh hotels. You have sex – a lot.

Then a baby comes along. The wonderful girl you dated changes overnight into a mother. You are no longer number one. You are not the most important one in her world anymore.

She chooses to stay at home all day and night. She doesn't want to go out anymore, but you still want to go out and party. She doesn't see any point in putting on those flimsy, low-cut dresses anymore or wearing tight jeans and skimpy tops. They all stay hanging in the wardrobe. Her hairdresser sees very little of her. She replaces her high-fashion clothes with baggy, scruffy jogging trousers, as she spends most of her day on her hands and knees, playing with the baby.

Her perfume is replaced with the smell of baby sick and stale food. Her hair and make-up is put on hold – what's the point in painting your nails when you spend most of the day washing dishes and clearing up. Her slim figure and perfect skin have been through the wars of childbirth.

Her friends don't ask her out to those parties anymore because they know she is always tired. They don't come round because they know she's always busy. Her conversation stoops to baby talk and what's on children's television these days.

You end up seeing more of her mother than you ever did before because she is constantly around, arranging and re-arranging things and giving advice on everything. She becomes your partner's best friend and you become, well, just part of the furniture.

The showroom house you used to live in, which was always kept tidy and perfectly clean, now becomes a children's play area. The only friends who do come round have got kids. Everything has to be moved: your treasured CD collection and your sporting trophies are now in a box ready for the loft. You can never find anything. You've stopped looking for the remote control. If you smoke, you have to spend most of your time in the garden. The dog you love so much is locked up in the downstairs utility room and stops getting his daily run on the beach. The exotic food you are used to in the evening becomes a microwaved ready meal.

When you get home after a hard day's work, supper is never ready and your suit very quickly gets covered in baby sick. The thought of having a beer when you get in is dismissed; she doesn't want alcohol around the baby. The programme on TV you have been following for years is now too violent around baby and you're left sitting at home at half past eight by yourself as your wife and baby are off to bed. And don't ever mention sex. She's too tired; she's just not in the mood.

If you do ever go out, her conversation is centred on how hard it is staying at home, looking after a baby. The friends you used to have who haven't got children now find you both extremely boring.

As a result, you start to go out two or three times a week and have fun with your mates. Most of them are single. Perhaps you go to a club, drink far too much alcohol, chat up some girls – just to make sure you can still do it. You can – and wallop! You spend the night with one of them and stagger home in the early hours of the morning, with your shirt on inside out, smelling of a bar and some girl's cheap perfume.

Boy gets bored, girl gets bored and hurt. And that's it: couple split up – another number for the government's figures at the Office for National Statistics. I know this is an exaggerated scenario, but I am sure there are a few home truths here.

Not so long ago, I saw a funny story going around on some of the social media sites. It was very similar to the scenario above. It went something like this:

A man came home from work and found his three children outside, still in their pyjamas, playing in the mud, with empty food boxes and wrappers strewn around garden. The door of his partner's car was open, as was the front door to the house. There was no sign of the dog. Walking in the door, he found his house in chaos. A lamp had been knocked over and the throw rug was against one wall. In the front room, the TV was blaring out the cartoon channel, and the room was strewn with toys and various items of clothing. In the kitchen, dishes filled the sink, breakfast food was spilled on the counter, the fridge door was wide open, dog food was all over the floor, a broken glass lay under the table and a small pile of sand was spread by the back door. He quickly headed up the stairs, stepping over toys and piles of clothes, looking for his partner. He was worried she might be ill, or that something serious had happened. He was met with a small trickle of water as it made its way out the bathroom door. As he peered inside, he found wet towels, scummy soap and more toys strewn over the floor. Miles of toilet paper lay in a heap and toothpaste had been smeared over the mirror and walls. As he rushed to the bedroom, he found his partner still curled up in bed in her pyjamas, reading a novel. She looked up at him, smiled and asked how his day had been. He looked at her bewildered and asked, "What happened here today?" She smiled again and answered, "You know every day when you come home from work and you ask me what in the world I do all day?" "Yes," he replied. Then she answered, "Well, today I didn't do it." It may be a funny story, but it is what happens in reality.

I had a look on the Internet to find out what was going on in relationships these days. It seems that many non-married couples and single parents claim that they have had a child by accident; it had not been planned. In my opinion, they have been totally irresponsible. The female pill is readily available nowadays, unlike in the 1960s. It was available to married woman in 1961, but single women had to wait until 1967 before they could get it.

And there is no excuse from the man's point-of-view either because condoms are everywhere. Condoms were available in the 1960s, but, as I said earlier, most men didn't know how to get them or use them, and they were extremely uncomfortable. Nowadays, you can't get away from condom machines. They are everywhere – supermarkets, toilets, pubs. Come on guys, it's a fashion statement down there these days; there is no real excuse not to wear one. The choice is endless: material (latex, polyurethane, polyisoprene or lambskin); lubrication (lubricated, non-lubricated and spermicidally lubricated); size (small, medium and large); texture (ultra thin, ultra sensitive, high sensation, extra strength, thick, ribbed and studded); novelty flavours (anything you can think of is available!); and colours (all the colours of the rainbow, including glow-in-the-dark ones!). There really is no excuse these days for an unwanted baby.

According to the government's figures, it is usually the dad who doesn't stick around, leaving the mum to rear the kids by herself. I think a lot of men think sex is just a bit of fun. The animal instinct takes over, and they think it's manly to score. Many men boast about how many girls they have had sex with.

But my initial thoughts were about the children and what life is like for them living without a dad. The statistics tell us there are many thousands of children in the UK being brought up without a dad. So why are dads so important? Some woman will argue they are not. Personally, I think it is important for a child to have a father around – perhaps it is because I am male. Nevertheless, reading the statistics really made me think about the importance of having us dads around.

I have read that a dad's playfulness can help children develop motor skills, hand-to-eye coordination, balance and confidence. Some child studies show that a dad's rough-and-tumble play helps children develop social and emotional experiences, which prepares them for school and for life – for example, learning to be confident, taking turns, acting as the leader, shrugging off unimportant things and dealing with bullying, both physical and mental.

I also think that men who are active fathers gain in their ability to understand themselves and others much better. Plus, just look at the health benefits you gain by taking your kids out to play.

Okay, so we dads can sometimes be a bit rowdy and loud. Some people might say this fulfils a vital role in a child's social, physical and intellectual development. "Dad's here – it's party time!" Then again, we've all heard that old saying "Just you wait till your father gets home!"

As I searched the Internet for information on why couples have unplanned babies, I noticed a recurring theme that unsettled me. There were many references to couples being drunk and not being aware of their responsibilities: "I was so drunk – I didn't care. I forgot all about contraception. I didn't think it would happen to me."

I am not meaning to preach; after all, I am fully aware that I was conceived after an unmarried couple's night out dancing to a top jazz band, an intimate meal, far too much wine, then a night of passionate, unprotected sex.

The thing that is different these days is that girls are keeping their babies. The families are helping more and, of course, my old chestnut, they are now being looked after by the state.

Back in the 1980s, there was a strong storyline in an extremely popular BBC soap programme called *Eastenders*. In the story, a young single girl becomes pregnant and the programme seemed to convey that it was acceptable to have a baby as a single mum. For months, the storyline was about how to declare poverty and homelessness to the council/government, in order to claim benefits and social support. This television programme was seen by millions of people, and I think it started a new generation of "looked-after" single mums.

The character's name was Theresa Mary Smith. She arrived in the series in March 1985. The story was that she had previously toured with a punk rock group and had slept with one of the members of the band. She was forced to quit when she became pregnant. Mary was originally from Stockport but moved to London when she became pregnant because she wanted to escape her overbearing family, who viewed her lifestyle with disgust and contempt.

Mary is young, has little money and virtually no experience. She finds it extremely difficult to bring up her baby, Annie. She cannot read and, as a result, she makes mistakes with her daughter's welfare: Annie is nearly harmed when Mary gives her the wrong dosage of medication. Unwilling to listen to anyone's advice, Mary turns to drugs and prostitution, stripping in clubs for money. In the series, she was labelled by some as a loose woman and by others as a hero for trying to bring up her child on her own.

On screen Mary is an incredibly irresponsible mother; almost every other character in the series has a turn at looking after Annie at some stage. They take pity on Mary and are willing to help her out, which she regularly uses to her advantage. One night, Mary leaves Annie at home alone, and she nearly dies in a fire.

The story has many twists and turns, but what it revealed was her dealings with the local authorities and social services. It was a huge storyline at the time. I remember the punk music movement was at its height back then. The programme gave mixed views on single parenting. It portrayed the difficulties of being a single mother, but it also glamorised it, in as much as the mother was rebelling against her parents and authority by bringing up a child as a single mum. I believe that the programme made it fashionable, almost desirable, to become a single mum. Many people were encouraged by it – including people I am very close to.

There was a second storyline in *Eastenders* around about the same time, which had a similar theme. The story was about the tough, feisty and very determined Michelle Fowler. When she is sixteen, she discovers she is pregnant. Despite pressure from her family, Michelle refuses to have an abortion and to name the father, even to her best friend, Sharon. She is adamant that she is keeping her baby. Speculation persists as to the identity of the father, but he is eventually revealed as Den Watts, Sharon's thirty-nine-year-old father. Michelle had turned to Den for sympathy during a difficult time and after a few drinks they'd had a one-night stand. Den promises to provide financial support for his child and keep its paternity a secret. Michelle spends the early part of her role in the series struggling with the hardships of being a pregnant teenager. She turns to a friend, Lofty, and uses him for comfort. He falls in love with her, proposes marriage and offers to adopt baby Vicki.

In short, Den talks her out of the marriage and she ditches Lofty at the altar. Later that year, she changes her mind again, and Lofty whisks her away for a secret wedding. But it does not go smoothly. Michelle grows tired of Lofty, who puts pressure on her to let him adopt Vicki legally and have another baby. Michelle doesn't like either idea; however, after an ill-fated attempt to elope with Den, she settles for an unhappy life with Lofty and ends up pregnant with Lofty's baby.

Lofty is overjoyed and, against Michelle's wishes, tells everyone about Michelle's pregnancy. Michelle retaliates by quietly having a private abortion, funded by Den, who doesn't want Lofty to adopt Vicki, his daughter. A devastated Lofty physically attacks Michelle in front of her family. The marriage dissolves, Lofty leaves the series and Den dies. Michelle goes on to have many relationships, demonstrating, perhaps, that another man can love and help look after her baby.

Michelle became central to the programme and was the focus of a controversial storyline. Press interest in the show escalated to record levels as journalists continuously tried to guess who had fathered her baby. Extra security was needed as they filmed the storyline.

So why was there such interest in this storyline? It seemed to promote teenage pregnancy and give approval for having an abortion if things don't work out. I'm not sure about the facts, but it wouldn't surprise me if there had been a rise in the amount of teenage pregnancies as a result of the programme.

The media – both television and radio – are so influential in areas such as this. In 1983, around the same time as these storylines hit the UK headlines, Madonna, an American singer-songwriter and queen of pop, released a single called "Papa Don't

Preach". The lyrics included the following: "Papa don't preach, I'm in trouble deep, Papa don't preach, I've been losing sleep, but I made up my mind, I'm keeping my baby, I'm gonna keep my baby, mmm …"

The song, written by Brian Elliot with additional lyrics by Madonna, is about teenage pregnancy. Madonna takes the voice of a confused teenager who wants advice from her father at a difficult time. In a 2009 interview with *Rolling Stone* magazine, she said: "It just fits right in with my own personal zeitgeist of standing up to male authorities, whether it's the pope, or the Catholic Church, or my father and his conservative, patriarchal ways."

The line "I've made up my mind, I'm keeping my baby" caused anti-abortion groups to praise Madonna and abortion-rights groups to criticise her. Madonna, who refused to take a stance on the issue, called this "a message song that everyone is going to take the wrong way".

Well, Madonna, I think thousands of girls at the time took it the way it sounds: that it is right to keep your baby, whatever the circumstances.

Shortly after its release, the song caused heated discussions about its lyrical content. While groups opposed to abortion saw it as a positive message, women's organisations and others in the family planning field criticised Madonna for encouraging teenage pregnancy – not just me then!

I think in today's world we just have to live with change. I can't help comparing the situation today with how it was in the 1960s, when Billie had me. Billie was never given the choice to "make up her mind and keep her baby".

Chapter 14

It really upset me to think I had hurt Geoff's wife. That phone call must have been extremely hard for her to make. I could think of no other way of telling her. I had been sensitive. I hadn't made a big fuss about it. After all, a couple of hours earlier, I had just discovered that my biological father had died and I was never going to meet him, so I was sad even before the call. I was left knowing I had hurt her and that Geoff had died. She was left with thoughts of him having been a deceitful, lying, secretive and unfaithful husband. She hadn't actually said that, but I could imagine that was probably what she was thinking after our phone call.

I think it would have been better had I been able to talk to her face-to-face, but I was on a phone mission to find out information. Besides, I had already told one of her relatives who I was and what information I had. I tried to imagine what she was going through, now she was older in her years. She had never remarried – she told me that – so she was probably an elderly widow, living in what I saw as a "remembrance shadow" of her beloved husband.

The walls of her house were probably covered with photographs: their wedding, them on holidays, him as a small child with his parents, their house in Australia. His framed medical certificates would have been carefully placed on top of cabinets. The sideboards were probably filled with things they had bought on holiday to remind them of all the wonderful places they had been together. Her bedside drawers would be filled with his cuff links, his watch, his wedding ring and the boat ticket stubs from their long one-way haul to Australia.

I could just imagine her walking around the house, crying hysterically, thinking why? Why had he had an affair? Why had he not told me? Why had he kept it such a secret? I realised he had kept a huge thing from her. She may now be wondering what else he had kept secret. She must also be asking herself whether anyone else knows. She must be questioning why they hadn't told her when Geoff had died. Was she now feeling paranoid that the whole family had been keeping a secret from her?

I think I was turning into an alcoholic by this stage. All I could think about was five o'clock. That was the time I would have my first drink. I had started to hide bottles so that no one really knew how much I was drinking. All of this searching and discovery was really getting to me. I suppose I'd thought it was going to be a fantastic, soul-searching, spiritual experience. Instead, it was getting very dark and sad. I felt I was taking in too much information; I was digging too deeply into the past and was hurting myself emotionally. Most of my findings were not happy, and I was spending a lot of my time in tears.

I wanted to phone Geoff's wife back, but what was I going to say? Sorry for upsetting you; sorry for my call; sorry for being your husband's son; sorry he didn't tell you.

I took a phone call that evening from someone saying she was Geoff's brother's daughter – a lady called Lesley. She introduced herself to me as my new cousin. She was fascinated by the news as she'd been collating the Boyce family tree. I had obviously added an interesting angle to her research! She was also a carer and very close family friend of Jayne, Geoff's wife.

It was obvious that they had talked; she knew all about my phone call. I think Jayne had phoned her straight after our conversation, perhaps to ask her whether she knew anything about me. In a very sympathetic way, she explained the effect my phone call had had on Jayne. Apparently, she was feeling very angry, not with me but with Geoff.

She was feeling angry that her loving husband of all these years had not told her anything about the baby and had lied to her for so long. She told me Jayne had taken all the pictures of him off the walls in her house and had put them away in drawers.

I could completely understand her anger about not having been told, but it hurt me to hear that Geoff's pictures – those loving memories she had of him – were now a reminder of his deceit and had been thrown into the darkness. In some strange way, I started to feel slightly protective over him.

I explained to Lesley that I was feeling very guilty; she told me not to be. I asked if I could send Jayne some flowers as an apology for my outburst. She said it was a very nice thought but, no, it wasn't the right time and that I should just let her think about this. I agreed.

Lesley asked, "Are you sure your information is correct and you are talking about the right person?" I repeated the information I had: his full name, occupation, old address, date of birth, hair colour, salary at the time – everything I had said to Jayne.

She did believe me; I could tell – or at least she had a very open mind to the idea. She said, "Geoff went away a lot after his daughter died. He was helping a friend with some maintenance work on his house around the time you were conceived. He was very upset when his daughter died. He loved children and was very good with them. You know so much information about Geoff. I do believe you; you sound sincere."

I told her I felt so guilty and apologised for my outburst. She kept saying that I had done nothing wrong, that I was the innocent party in all of this. It didn't feel like that.

Lesley said she had known Geoff very well. He used to play with her a lot when she was a little girl. It was obvious she had been very fond of him. She continued, "He was a really friendly person, liked by all the family. He was very particular about his appearance. I can remember he had starched collars on his shirts. He was an occupational therapist and was very good at his job. He was a real people person. Children always went to him and liked him. Richard, my brother, and I had a wonderful time with him. He would tell us stories. I am sure they weren't true but we would listen enthralled. Your dad was very good at sports. I think he coached athletics at one stage. When he and Jayne went to Australia we obviously lost touch a bit. He worked with disabled people, you know."

I said I was a people person, too. I told her that I had two children of my own, had always been good at sport and was quite particular about my appearance, just like Geoff. I also mentioned that, when looking for Geoff, I had written to a lady who had been a neighbour years ago, and she had mentioned that they had been thinking of moving to Australia.

Lesley told me Geoff had six brothers and one sister. "You know, you're part of a huge family," she said. "You have loads of cousins and relatives. I'm making up the Boyce family tree at the moment. I must add you."

Until fairly recently, I had known only two blood relatives – my two sons; I'd just been told that, actually, I had bloody loads.

She asked me about my family and where I lived. I told her; she seemed to know Devon very well. She and her husband often came this way with their caravan and drove through my village. She thought it was a lovely part of the country. I told her I had been living there for many years and loved it.

She wanted to know about my parents and whether I'd had a good life. I explained that I'd been very happy and that my parents were great. She wondered if they knew about my searching and whether they approved. I explained that, although they knew, they were worried about me and that "approved" was the wrong word to describe how they felt about it.

Lesley went on to explain to me that some of her family had questioned my intentions – they basically didn't believe me.

Apparently, the phone hadn't stopped ringing for the last few hours. I said that it was understandable. She said, "The news is going through the family like wild fire. Everyone is talking about you." The woman I first talked to, a relation of Lesley's, had obviously phoned loads of people with my news straight after putting the phone down on me. Lesley said, "She's a bit of a gossip. I think she's enjoying the drama of telling everyone."

Lesley went on to tell me a lot about the Boyce family history, but it was too much to take in. We both agreed we would have to meet very soon. I said I had a lot of official paperwork relating to Geoff, which would back up my story. I felt it was important that she see some of it, and she agreed. Lesley explained that she was the main communicator in the family; everyone goes to her for information. She is the one who keeps everybody updated on everything. She gets on with all of the family and keeps in contact with all of them. She seemed really excited about discovering me – excited she had a new cousin. She welcomed me into the family.

She asked if I had found my mother. I corrected her. "My blood mother – yes. Unfortunately, she had passed over." She asked me if I meant that she had passed away. I hesitated and confirmed that she had and that I had just been to her funeral a couple of weeks earlier. She said she was very sorry and offered her condolences. I went on to tell her briefly the story about Billie and Geoff – how they had met at a hospital ball and had known each other for a couple of years; how Billie had died and how I was just two years too late to meet her.

Lesley questioned how I had been at her funeral, so I explained that I had met a friend of Billie's, who had kept the ashes for me, and we'd had a special second service at Woking crematorium so that I could be present.

Lesley stopped me in my tracks and said, "Woking crematorium?" "Yes," I replied. She continued, "You must keep this too yourself. If any other family members contact you, please, don't tell them about Woking." I asked why, and she told me that she would explain when we met. She wanted us to meet very soon.

Then she went on to say the words I had heard before, "Do you want to see a picture of him? I have lots of them."

I thought, *Oh, my god, here we go again!* But, of course, I didn't say that. I thanked her and said that I would love to see them. After all, it was what I wanted. I started to get excited about seeing them. This was what my search was all about: finding answers, seeking relatives, looking at photographs, discovering who I was and where I'd come from – wasn't it?

We exchanged email addresses, and I also gave her the website address for my band. That way, she would be able to see pictures of me, too, and see that I was a musician. As we ended the call, she said she couldn't wait to send me the pictures and would ring me again the following day. She then welcomed me into her family once more.

I felt much better about that call to Lesley. She had genuinely believed my story. She had been very friendly, and she certainly hadn't made me feel bad about contacting Jayne. It didn't take away the guilt, but it helped.

I sat at my computer and stared at the screen, waiting, just as I had done with Penny previously. Every word of the phone call with Jayne was going through my mind. I had really hurt Geoff's wife with my news, and to hear she had taken down all of his pictures made me feel even worse. I had also just been told that I was part of a huge family and had loads of new cousins. I didn't feel comfortable about that at all.

But are these people really my family? I suppose they are in a way. I really hadn't been expecting that when I'd started my search. I thought I would meet my blood parents and that would be it. I'd never thought any further than that. Lesley kept mentioning she was my cousin and that I had loads of them.

I immediately thought of my real cousins, the ones I had grown up with, the ones I had shared family holidays with. They were my proper cousins. What the hell was I going to say to them when I spoke to them next? "Oh, by the way, you know how you're my cousin, well, I've been researching for my biological parents, and I've just found out I have loads more cousins, just like you." I didn't think that would go down very well at all.

I didn't know who these new people were. It was a real head spinner, and I felt very guilty and angry with myself. What was I doing? I had just opened a huge can of disillusionment.

Lesley had also told me that some members of her family thought I was lying and had made this whole thing up. So, now I was a liar in some people's eyes. I guess they thought I was looking for some sort of family inheritance; you hear of it all the time.

I reached for another large scotch; it was helping me to feel less sensitive to things and a little less emotional. When I had received Penny's pictures of Billie, I'd felt really hurt to start with. Was I really ready to be hurt again?

Emails started to come in. Before opening the attachments, I read the message from Lesley:

Dear Steve,

I am Lesley, niece of Geoff Boyce. He was my father's youngest brother and a much-loved uncle to my older brother Richard and me.

I feel I must ask the question – do you think there is any doubt that we are related? On your website you certainly seem to favour the Boyce look. Jayne keeps asking if it is true – I can only say that I think it is. She keeps going over and over the events and times. She has such a job thinking that Geoff betrayed her. I am hoping that time will heal a little bit.

In the meantime, can you think of particular questions that you would like answered? I will look out more photos for you.

I hope you can enjoy the knowledge that you have many more relatives – I don't know if that is good or bad – but be assured we are all quite nice people and there aren't any skeletons in the cupboards – perhaps I shouldn't have said that – there might well be, I suppose, but none that I know of.

It is such a shock to hear that Geoff had another child. When their daughter, Jennifer, died of cystic fibrosis after a long illness, Jayne and Geoff did struggle but came through the tragedy. Although they didn't have any more children, they had a good marriage, and Jayne was very upset when he died. He adored children and was very good with them, which is why she is struggling with the fact that he kept your birth to himself – presumably not to hurt anyone. The death of their beloved daughter (a little dark-haired girl) affected them deeply. He must have been tortured with guilt regarding you. Your news has hit her for six, and she will need some time to accept the past.

My brother and I would like to meet you – our new cousin – very soon. From the pictures on the Internet of you performing in your band, I can see how much you resemble our father in his younger years – handsome days.

Enclosed are some pictures of your father.

My husband and I are planning to come and meet you next week if you're free.

Yours
Lesley

I opened the attachments: Geoff in the Navy, Geoff in the fire service during the war, Geoff with Jayne at a party. Then, a large and very detailed high-resolution one of his face, taken when he was just a few years older than me. I saw the resemblance instantly. I was in floods of tears again.

Geoff's pictures made a lot more sense to me than Billie's. To start with, I looked like him. My facial character lines were the same; the forehead lines were identical; our skin tone and hair were the same. It was very obvious; he was my biological father.

If you were to put both of us in the same room, you could easily tell we were related. I put our two pictures together on the computer – me at nearly fifty and Geoff in his mid-fifties. Was this what all the fuss was about – finding people who looked like me?

Don't get me wrong; it was good to see a picture of my biological father, to see what he looked like and to see the resemblance. But it felt so wrong; my real father was still alive, and he had been so good to me – and good for me. He had been a fantastic dad, better than anyone else ever could be, and I love him so much.

So what the hell was I doing with my silly, selfish searching – looking for another dad? It all seemed a bit pointless. And it hurt.

Chapter 15

The news was travelling fast around the Boyce family: one of the more popular, successful and admired members of the family had had a secret affair and has son.

Once again, my website stats were going ballistic. I was getting hundreds of hits. My pictures were being shared and downloaded. Who is this person claiming to be Geoff's son? Does he look like Geoff? Does he look like a Boyce? Where has he come from and what does he want?

My website pictures, which I'd put onto the Internet to promote the band, get us work and sell CDs, were now being scrutinised. They were being analysed by people looking for a likeness to Geoff. Although there were still lots of hits from Brighton (including from the property Billie lived in, which I couldn't understand), the statistics now showed many hits from Australia. I could see that people had been downloading my music and looking repeatedly at the site in the very early hours of the morning. Then I realised, of course, that Australia has a different time zone to the UK. Lesley hadn't told me that there were other relatives living out there.

The following day, I received an email from someone in Australia – a girl called Rose. She said she'd got my email address through my website. The Australian jungle drums had obviously been pounding loudly that night. She had heard the family news: Geoff had had an affair, Geoff had been unfaithful, Geoff had been keeping a secret from all of us, and we have a new member in our family claiming to be his son. Her email read:

Hi Steve,

I am your cousin Rose from down under. Just heard through the family gossip grapevine that you have discovered your roots, so to speak. Uncle Geoff, your dad, was my favourite uncle. He passed away when I was a teenager. He was living in Sydney at the time. My dad, your uncle Peter, was a jazz guitarist in the 1950s. He moved to Australia, played in a few bands here, met my mum and the rest is history.

We are really excited to have you in the family. If you are ever in Australia, we would love to meet you. Dad is eighty-two years old. He is over the moon that you are also a jazz muso [musician] and is very proud of you.

I am the youngest cousin in Australia, and I work with animals – vet nursing. I have two sisters. Geoff and Jayne had a daughter, who unfortunately died. They didn't have any other kids. Geoff always told my mum he wanted to adopt a child. Mum told me that, when she thinks about it, he probably meant you.

I have attached a few pictures. The one with a jazz band is my dad in the 50s. He is the guitarist on the right. I have listened to your music and think it's wonderful. You are very talented.

When he lived in the UK, my dad, your uncle Peter, played with Ted Heath many times around 1946 at the Hammersmith Palais de Danse. He played a lot with Edmundo Ros and his Orchestra. He also had a regular gig with a dance band at the Rendezvous Ballroom and often played with Felix Mendelssohn's Hawaiian Serenaders.

While in the UK, Geoff and Peter were great friends with legendary guitarist Bert Weedon. I think they were introduced when Peter played with the Ted Heath Orchestra.

In the 1950s, when he moved to Australia, he regularly played and recorded with Jim Vickers-Willis, a top square-dancing band. In

1954, Louis Armstrong asked him to play with him at his Melbourne
Town Hall gigs. His guitarist or pianist was ill, so Peter stepped in.

He mentioned to me that he regularly played on the In Melbourne
Tonight *show with Bert Newton and Graham Kennedy. [This was a*
popular variety show, which was broadcast every night.]

He had to give most of his jazz playing work up when my big sister
was born. He found the combination of having to leave Mum alone
and the constant travel too stressful and too costly.

…

Love Rose (your new little cuz)

Rose enclosed more pictures of Geoff: a family Christmas
gathering, Geoff on a motorbike, Geoff and her dad drinking
whisky (I liked that one) and a picture of her dad playing guitar
in a jazz band.

I had seen a resemblance to Geoff when Lesley's pictures came
in, but seeing Rose's dad was uncanny. I could instantly see a
resemblance to me. His facial bone structure was the same as
mine and his hair and eyes had a remarkable resemblance.

The way he was looking at his instrument while playing was
so similar to the way I do it. Was he the one I had taken my
musical gift from? Who knows, but he certainly has all the right
qualifications for it.

It was lovely hearing from Rose. We ended up having lots of
private chats on the Internet. She didn't once ask me if I was sure
about my relationship with the family. She didn't doubt it at all. I
will always thank her for that. We were both genuinely excited
that we'd found each other and often chatted about our lives.

I couldn't believe it. I was so excited and proud to discover
that my uncle had played with Louis Armstrong. The great Louis

Armstrong needs no introduction; he is simply the greatest jazz musician who walked on the planet. During a world tour in 1964, he stopped off in Australia for a series of memorable concerts in Melbourne. The musicians who travelled with him – and the ones with whom Peter would have played – were Jewel Brown (vocals), Trummy Young (trombone), Arvell Shaw (bass), Joe Darensbourg (clarinet), Billy Kyle (piano) and Danny Barcelona (drums). I guess Billy may have fallen ill, and Peter had to take over the chords on guitar. There is an album and DVD recorded at the time in Melbourne, but I don't think Peter gets a mention in the credits. I am not actually sure whether he played on it. The album is called *Louis Armstrong: Live in Australia*. I must order it and have a look.

I'm a huge fan of his and have been listening to his records since I was a little boy. When people of my generation talk of their first musical influences or the first records that made an impact on their lives, they usually mention The Beatles or Elvis Presley. Yes, I was a fan of Elvis, but it was Satchmo (Louis Armstrong) and Frank Sinatra who caught my attention at a very early age and who shaped my style of jazz playing today.

Ted Heath led Britain's greatest post-war big band, recording more than one hundred albums and selling over twenty million records. His band was considered the most famous and successful band in Britain at the time. His musicians were regular poll winners in the *Melody Maker* and *New Musical Express (NME)*, both leading music newspapers. They regularly played at the London Palladium and Hammersmith Palais. I was also a fan. My parents talked about going to see them and dancing the night away when they were first courting in London. I wonder if Peter was playing in the band on one of the nights they danced there.

The connection with Edmundo Ros and his Orchestra was interesting. Ros was a Trinidadian musician, vocalist, arranger and bandleader, who made his career in Britain. He directed a highly popular Latin American orchestra and had an extensive

162

recording career. There is reference on the Internet that Peter played on his 1949 classic song "The Wedding Samba", which sold three million 78-RPM records. It also appeared on the soundtrack of the 2006 British romantic comedy drama film *A Good Year*. It is a superb track.

Felix Mendelssohn (not to be confused with the German composer) had one of Britain's most popular Hawaiian style bands in the 30s and 40s. They were heard regularly on the radio and TV and made a long and fascinating series of recordings. They used many guitarists in the band, one being Peter. Bet he had some fun in that band with all the glamorous girls in their skimpy grass skirts.

So, Geoff and Peter had been friends with Bert Weedon. He introduced the guitar to millions, including Hank Marvin, The Beatles, Brian May and Eric Clapton, to name a few. He played with the greats, including Frank Sinatra, Judy Garland, Tony Bennett and Stéphane Grappelli, and we all bought his inspiring and well-known book *Play In A Day*.

Jim Vickers–Willis dominated the Australian square-dancing boom of the 1950s. He and the band played to thousands of dancers at one time, and his square dances were broadcast all over Australian radio and television. Peter was his regular guitarist for years and can be heard on many of his recordings. The music could be described as country but had a very strong jazz influence. A lot of the numbers Peter and the band played were songs my band do now, such as "Five Foot Two Eyes Of Blue", "I'm Nobody's Sweetheart Now" and "When Your Smiling", to name a few. I have just ordered some of his albums this afternoon. The track "Alabama Jubilee" was one of their most famous tunes.

In Billie's letters, she mentioned that she and Geoff used to go to the Hammersmith Palais. I wonder if Geoff went there knowing his brother was in the band? He probably got them tickets. There was also a mention in one of her letters about dancing at the Palais the night I was conceived.

I spent days and days researching these artists and listening to their music, trying to pick out the guitar parts that my uncle Peter would have played on. We jazz musicians can dissect a piece of music; we can easily break down the recording so that we can hear what each individual instrument is doing – something that the average listener struggles to do.

Discovering all this information made me feel good. I was really proud of my newfound relations. It was great to know my searching was, at last, making me happy and I was enjoying my findings. It made such a difference to how I viewed my search. It also made me feel good knowing that Peter had told Rose he was over the moon about me being a jazz musician – or "muso" as he had called me – and that he was proud of me and had listened to my recordings. Earlier I mentioned I was a bit uncomfortable about having new so-called family members. I felt okay about this one and, of course, about Rose.

A couple of days later the phone rang again. It was Lesley, Geoff's niece. She wanted to arrange a meeting and said she was looking for a hotel near where I lived. I agreed it was a great idea. I recommended a hotel where she and her husband could stay, and she went ahead and booked a room for an overnight stay.

I could completely understand that Lesley wanted to have a look at some of the paperwork I had, especially the official court adoption paperwork with Geoff's name on it. She explained again that some members of her family didn't believe that there was another Boyce out there and were unwilling to accept that Geoff had had an affair all those years ago. Lesley mentioned that various family members had been in touch with her and had told her that they'd looked at my website and could see a strong resemblance to Geoff. It appeared, however, that some of the others needed persuading. I think Lesley believed me, but she was being sent on a family mission to find out more and return with the evidence.

I'd arranged to meet Lesley and her husband at a very nice hotel, situated on a dramatic cliff top, overlooking the sea, close to my village. I arrived early and sat in the car waiting for them to arrive. I was nervous. I was not sure what to expect. Would she be angry with me? Was I on trial? It certainly felt like it. I had made photocopies of various letters and documents proving who I was and what had actually happened nearly fifty years ago. I wanted to show her the proof and let her keep the copies to show the others, who were suspicious of my motives. Geoff's name was on many of the legal papers, and Billie mentioned him many times in her letters.

Her car pulled up, and she instantly recognised me. She got out of her car, gave me a big hug and introduced herself as my new cousin.

Lesley had her husband with her, and I had my family for support. They wanted to be there for me. Lesley had sweets for the kids, which always goes down well, and I brought her flowers. My family made their introductions and decided to go for a walk on the beach, leaving Lesley and her husband with me so we could talk.

The first thing I did was to explain a little of my searching process, and then I showed her the documents that backed up my story. I genuinely think Lesley was pleased and excited about having a new cousin. I don't think she needed convincing; she was there as the family representative. She and her husband had no doubt who I was. She said I had Geoff's looks, his skin tone, his facial features and some of his mannerisms – if that is possible.

She mentioned that the way I held and smoked my cigarette was the exact way Geoff used to do it. Likewise with the way I sat and the way I held and drank a cup of tea. I don't know how much of that was true. How can someone take on board characteristics of a person they have never met? But he was my biological father, I suppose.

We sat and talked for hours. She told me again about her large family. Geoff had six brothers and a sister, and her father was a great friend of Geoff's when he was living in the UK – his favourite brother, in fact, so she had spent many family gatherings with him and knew him very well. She spoke highly of my blood father, saying he was a very clever and kind man. He was well respected and loved. I enjoyed hearing those things.

A few days before the visit, Lesley had spent a sleepless night writing out all the family history for me. She said she was so excited about hearing my news that she just had to put pen to paper and couldn't sleep till she had finished.

She presented me with nine pages of A4, all handwritten, giving me details of the Boyce family going back to 1857. I was given details of everyone associated with my new blood family, their marriage details, occupations, children's names and, in most cases, death dates and details of how they had died.

I must say, it was fascinating, although overwhelming. I knew details of my real parents' history but only really comprehended it as far back as my parent's parents, because I had met and shared time with them, I suppose. I had never really dwelt on the past that much until now. Why should I? I had no real blood past to speak of.

Geoff's details were of most interest to me. He was born on 3 January 1925, and he died on 23 September 1983. I found it interesting that my real father's birthday is 23 September. Geoff died of ischaemic heart disease, emphysema and carcinoma of the prostate with metastasis. He died at the age of fifty-eight, so, if my medical genes are the same as my blood father's, I only have a few years left to live. What a thought!

They had one daughter, Jennifer Susan, born on 7 May 1956, who died of cystic fibrosis on 4 June 1959. She was only three years old and, if alive today, my half-sister would have been fifty-eight too.

I was reminded that Geoff had been a carrier of cystic fibrosis. I told her I had spoken to my doctor about it. It takes two to pass it on, and Billie was clear. It did make me wonder why Geoff had slept with Billie, knowing he carried the disease. I'm not sure the medical profession knew at the time that both partners must carry it to pass it on.

I learned that Geoff had worked in the fire service and had then joined the navy. Afterwards, whilst in England, he qualified as an occupational therapist and gained further qualifications in this field when he moved to Australia.

There was an entry in his mother's diary on 20 June 1939, saying that he had fractured his jawbone and had been sent to Guy's Hospital in London, where his jaw had been wired together. My real father often talked of Guy's Hospital. He had trained as a doctor and surgeon there, though not at that time.

I read that Geoff had had a mastoid operation and that he'd had a tattoo of a snake on his arm, which he'd had done whilst in the navy. He had regretted it afterwards and later had it removed, which had left a large scar on his arm. In November 1966, he'd emigrated with Jayne to Australia, and they had lived in a stunning one-bedroomed flat, which overlooked the sea in Dee Why, a suburb of northern Sydney in the state of New South Wales.

I was born in 1961, so he must have been living in the UK for around five years before leaving. I wonder if he kept in contact with Billie? He died in 1983 and was cremated in Australia – so far away from England. I'll probably never get the chance to visit his grave.

I was given a newspaper cutting of an article written by C. Nixon, the co-editor of the *Spastic's Workshop Magazine*, based in New South Wales, Australia. The journal printed a very warm piece about Geoff just after he died. Here is the transcript:

TRIBUTE TO A "BIG" MAN

Amongst the many flowers and flowering shrubs that help decorate the entrance to Centre Industries, there is a rose tree with a plaque alongside. Both tree and plaque stand in silent tribute to an Englishman. No, not some famous lord, but a physiotherapist who began work at C. I. some twenty years ago, and endeared himself to all who knew him.

Geoff Boyce died recently and, although to many such a tragedy was unthinkable, yet he had been beset by nagging illness for some time.

If ever a man devoted his entire energies to making the lot of the disabled less daunting, it was Geoff. Ever thinking of more inventions and modifications to achieve this end, one might regularly find him in his office, working on appliances which his fertile brain told him would make this or that task more simple for his C. P. "chums".

Even allowing for this, Geoff was ever ready to listen to the troubles – either physical or emotional – of his friends. To share in a laugh, or perhaps offer some sound advice.

I got to know Geoff Boyce pretty well over the years. That was my extreme good fortune. We exchanged theories on everything from science to International Cricket. Never once during that time did we argue, or find cause to so do. Nor did I hear him raise his well-modulated voice to anyone else. You see, Geoff was something very rare in this day and age. A complete gentleman.

To say The Spastics Centre will be the poorer for his passing would be something of an understatement. I shall miss him, as will many others at Centre Industries, though I am sure I will never forget that big, big man.

C Nixon, Co-editor

I started to do a bit of research on the place.

The Centre Industries factory, as it was called, was established in 1961. It used to be called the Spastic Centre and was founded in 1944 under the leadership of Neil and Audrey McLeod. In the early years of the war, the McLeods arrived in Sydney from Perth with their daughter, who had cerebral palsy. They were hoping to find treatment for their daughter and set up a centre for other parents in the same situation as them. Initially fourteen children attended, but by the end of the first year they had forty attending. Shortly afterwards, this number had grown to over two hundred in residence, with some three hundred people employed. The McLeods, Nixon and Geoff lived by the motto "Nothing is Impossible". Geoff worked with the McLeods to help launch the centre and would have been instrumental in helping to develop its popularity.

After more than six decades in business the Spastic Centre C.I. was encouraged to change its name, as in those days the word spastic had too many negative connotations. On 31 August 2010, a resolution to change the name of the organisation to Cerebral Palsy Alliance was made. The new name took effect on 8 February 2011. It was hoped that this change would enable them to achieve a stronger profile, with clarity of purpose and unambiguous focus on cerebral palsy. At the time of the relaunch, the Australian news headlines used a very controversial song by British band Ian Dury and the Blockheads. The song used was called "Spasticus Autisticus". So, by the sounds of it, Geoff was a very talented and caring man. I feel proud of him and his compassionate and creative achievements.

When searching for blood relatives, many people are rightly interested to find out about their medical history. As well as being given information about the Boyce family history, I was now in possession of their medical details, including causes of death. So, in addition to Geoff's ailments, I was now looking at emphysema, heart failure, cardiomyopathy, cystic fibrosis, strokes, lung problems, ventricular fibrillation, myocardial ischemia and rheumatoid arthritis. Oh my god! I wish I didn't know all this now!

Lesley had mentioned there was a hearing problem that ran in the family – it seemed it hadn't affected me, thank god. Lesley was very interested to know where my musical talent had come from. She had time to think about it before our meeting. She offered me several potential sources: one of Geoff's brothers played the banjo and had an artistic daughter who loved to paint; another dabbled with the keyboard; Geoff's sister's son was a DJ and played music; another brother had a large keyboard at home; and, of course, Peter Boyce was a very talented professional jazz guitarist, who had played with many famous musicians. I was able to enlighten Lesley about Peter's musical achievements. I now knew so much about them. I told her I had heard from Rose and that we had spent a lot of time chatting. She was okay about that.

So if I were to analyse where my genetic musical talent came from I would probably say Billie's mum, as she was a popular concert pianist, and Peter, Geoff's brother with his jazz bands. I must also thank my parents for recognising and nurturing the talent at a very early age.

I also discovered that many of the Boyce family had been buried at Woking Crematorium – the very place where Billie had asked to be laid to rest and where a lot of her family were also buried. I now understand why Lesley had been so defensive about this subject and had wanted me to keep it a secret, especially from Jayne.

I explained to Lesley that Billie had also chosen that place and that many members of her family were resting there too. This seemed so strange to me; loads of my blood relatives had been laid to rest in the same area – the same crematorium, all of them in the same town. They had lived all over the country, so why had they all end up in the same town? They had made their way from all over to be buried in, let's face it, the same field.

So many pictures and stories were exchanged that afternoon; I certainly learned a lot about Geoff and the vast Boyce family from that visit. It was really nice to meet Lesley and her husband. They were both very pleasant, understanding and sympathetic people, who had made me feel very relaxed and had welcomed me into their family.

I don't know why but just as they were leaving I told her very briefly about my spiritual experience with Billie. I must have sounded absolutely nuts. This nice new cousin of hers, whom she had just met, was barking mad. She seemed interested and didn't think it was that strange at all – or at least she appeared not to be too concerned. I also told her that, now I had found out that Geoff had died, I might get in touch with the medium again and go back to the spiritualist church.

Chapter 16

I still had Billie's ashes under the piano. The movements in the house were still going on – and were beginning to get to me a little. I'd found out who Billie was and had got to know a lot about her life – I'd even been to her funeral. I felt it was time for us both to move on. I needed to try to stop the, let's call them, occurrences happening. It was interesting to start with but, if I am being honest, I wanted a bit of privacy. Plus, it wasn't fair on the family.

I decided to make contact with my two little old ladies again, the ones who recommended this phenomena to me – if that's the right word for it. Perhaps they would know how to stop, or at least control, the presence of Billie in my house. Plus, I had a few unanswered questions for Geoff and was interested to know if the spiritualist lady was due in the area again. Stella and Connie knew how to get hold of this special lady.

I explained to them again about how things were moving around in my house and that I wanted it to stop. I also reminded them that Billie had been a spiritualist and that I had her crystals. They said they would have a think about it and phone me back. Sure enough, an hour or so later, the phone rang. They had spoken to a friend about it, and she had given them some advice.

My ladies told me to put Billie's ashes in my loft. I was to place the urn as high up in the house as I could and hang her crystals on a piece of string or chain directly above the urn – hang them from the rafters so they would dangle directly over the ashes without touching the urn. It sounded a bit crazy, but I was willing to try anything.

That afternoon I did just that, and I think it worked! So far I have had no movements or electricity problems; I no longer see shadows or feel any strange presence. It's a bit sad, but that's the way I wanted it. I don't feel bad in any way; she is still with me –

well, let's say her ashes are being kept safely in my house. She had told me, through the medium, not to put them in my garden or in any other place, so I had respected her wish. My blood mother was safely in my loft, and I knew that, if I really wanted to, I could bring her down at any time – you know, should I feel like having a little chat. That last line does make me sound totally crazy, but I felt it was an option if I wanted to. Had I had a reunion with my blood mother? It is so often talked about in the world of an adoptee. I would say, yes, I have – but not in the true sense of the word.

My little old ladies were right. It had worked. They also gave me a date in a couple of weeks' time for another meeting with the medium. This time it wasn't going to be at the church; they had made a private appointment with the same lady at their house for the three of us. They also had a few people they wanted to make contact with.

I still hadn't gone through all of Billie's personal possessions in great detail. There were lots of very interesting things in there, one of which was a selection of newspaper clippings she had kept from the days we were at Red Gables Mother and Baby Home. They were about Teresa, the girl who had abandoned her baby in a telephone box. There was a dusty brown envelope filled with old yellow clippings from evening newspapers with headlines such as "Baby abandoned", "Baby found" and "Mother reunited with baby". There was also another, more general, article about foundlings. I had never come across the word "foundling" until I read the story.

Foundlings are children abandoned, almost always by their mothers, very soon after birth. There is rarely any intention that the child should die, but the mother is usually in a mental state whereby she cannot act rationally, or else she is in a position where she feels unable to approach the social services for help.

The desperate girls normally choose their moment and place the babies very carefully. They are usually left somewhere where they will be found by a responsible person very soon after they are abandoned – places such as a hospital, a church or on the steps of the local newspaper. In many cases a telephone box is used, and the mother sometimes takes the telephone number of the box and phones it years later.

The article explained how poverty is often the root cause of child abandonment and talked about how people in cultures with poor social welfare systems are not always financially capable of taking care of a child. The article also related Teresa's abandonment of her child to the children's storybook *Snow White*, in which the child is actually abandoned by a servant who had been given orders to put the child to death.

I found the whole concept of foundlings interesting, so I decided to do a bit of research into it.

Foundling babies were a common occurrence historically. The statistics are changing all the time, but even today's figures indicate that it is still happening. Unfortunately, many of the parents are never traced, leaving their offspring with no name and no knowledge of their family. They don't even know their official birthdays. For some reason, of all the babies found dead, there are more boys than girls. Some people believe girls are tougher and more likely to survive exposure than boys. Who knows?

The children are often abandoned with birth tokens, cuddly toys, handkerchiefs, T-shirts, necklaces, scarves, etc. The reason for this is that the mother wants to make sure that the child can be identified in some small way.

I think that those people who were abandoned as babies back in the 1960s, and who are now adults, will have many more psychological problems than those of us who were adopted at that time. It must be difficult living with the knowledge that you had previously been thrown away or dumped in a dirty street corner. What makes it worse is not knowing whether you had been dumped there and left to die, or left there with some sort of hope that you would be found. It is thought that most of the mothers who abandoned their babies in this manner were very young; they were trying to keep their pregnancies a secret, possibly as the result of incest or rape. Not knowing your birthday must be a hard one to cope with as well as being a constant reminder of your abandonment.

Mothers, especially young ones, can become overwhelmed by the presence of a child growing inside them for nine months. When the baby is born, the distressed mother can lose contact with reality and experience post-natal depression or feelings of inadequacy. In some cases, mothers consider abandoning their child as an alternative to having an abortion. Perhaps they leave their baby believing the infant will have a chance of a better life, education and prospects with new parents.

I wondered why Billie had kept the articles on foundlings. She knew Teresa, of course; however, perhaps it was also because she was upset by how someone could just abandon a baby like that. It seems such a harsh thing to do, depriving the child of attachment or love.

By this stage in my search, I was becoming very interested in the whole concept of adoption and how the process has changed over the years. I already knew a lot about what happened in the 1960s, but I was being drawn in by present-day media headlines relating to adoption. It is still going on but in a very different way. I was keen to find out more about the current adoption process. I didn't want to approach someone who dealt with this in my area as I thought they might know Sue, the adoption manager who was dealing with my case. I wanted to keep both areas of my research separate. Also, I didn't want Sue to know I was thinking of writing my story.

I remembered that the previous year, whilst playing with my band at a wedding, I had met a lady who was an adoption manager. We'd got talking about adoption and she'd given me her card. She didn't deal with people like me, who were searching for their blood parents; her job was to seek out potential parents and promote the idea of adopting a child. There are people doing this job in regional government departments all over the UK. The government issues guidelines and rules about how it should be done, but, in my opinion, it is the managers and their staff who are playing god.

I knew that the adoption manager I had met at the wedding would be right up-to-date with the current adoption system, so I looked out her details and arranged a meeting. I had to travel quite far to see her, but it was worth it. After a long train journey and a taxi ride that seemed to take forever, I arrived at our meeting place. She remembered me and our previous conversation. She was pleased to see me again – I had obviously made an impression on her the day we first met.

I was utterly shocked by my meeting, on many levels. I am not going to mention her name or the area she covers for obvious reasons, but my meeting was a real eye-opener, which was perhaps fuelled by my own sensitivity and insecurity about being adopted.

I had prepared a list of questions, so I started at the beginning and asked her what type and age of children were available today and waiting for adoption. From that initial opener, our conversation flowed. I learned so much about the process, listened to heart-breaking examples and found myself questioning this new system.

There are very few babies available now. When I say very few, I mean nearly non-existent. The chance of getting a child a year old or up to eighteen months is, in her words, like gold dust. It just doesn't happen very often. The child is likely to be between five and ten years old. The reason that there are so few babies available is that the girls are keeping them nowadays. The system is so different today; the government supports single mums. They receive allowances and financial benefits. In many cases, they are even provided with a home. All of this with no negative stigma attached whatsoever. This is a very controversial subject, especially with the older generation. Many people ask why the British taxpayer should support girls who become pregnant and can't afford to look after their babies.

As we talked, I told her a bit about my story and why I was interested in how things operate these days. We both agreed that, if the girls of today knew how things had happened in the 1960s, they would be shocked. It would make them feel extremely grateful that they weren't living in that period. She firmly believed that if you can't afford children you shouldn't have them. I kind of agreed with her – I say "kind of" because, of course, I am adopted. I think my views were a bit selfish and distorted, but I could see things from her side too.

Billie couldn't afford to keep me so she was forced to put me up for adoption. It just wasn't fair back then. I was trying desperately to stop getting upset about girls having babies out of wedlock and not wearing wedding rings.

It was very hard to listen to the adoption manager describe the circumstances of the children who are adopted today. An extremely high percentage of them have been abused. Abused and neglected by their parents. She told me that the majority of them had been hurt in very cruel ways: bones broken by angry mothers and fathers, left in squalled conditions with no food or water; arms, hands and legs put in boiling water for restraint and punishment; cigarettes put out on the child's skin for crying too loudly; left on their own for days – the list goes on and on. It is horrific. I started to cry when she listed some of the things her waiting kids had gone through. How could people do this?

She went on to tell me drug and alcohol addiction play a huge part in this whole picture. Many children are coming into the system with parents so high and doped up they couldn't care less about their children. All they are interested in is getting that next hit, that next injection of heroin or that next bottle of vodka. All the family's money is being spent on these things, these abusive substances.

It is so sad but true; a massive proportion of the poor children who are available for adoption nowadays have so far in their short lives only ever experienced totally dysfunctional and fucked-up parents.

But there is another side. Some parents have learning difficulties and/or mental and physical problems. They have little or no concept that sex can produce a child – no understanding of contraception – and, when the baby arrives, have no idea of how they can cope or look after it. What's more, in some cases the baby may inherit the issues that the parents have – and the vicious circle continues.

In addition, some perfectly normal parents have a child who is born with physical abnormalities or learning issues, but they don't want the child because it is not what they expected or wanted. They can't or don't want to try to cope with bringing up a child who has physical or mental problems.

I know many parents who have children with difficulties of some sort or another. I know they sometimes struggle to have what we might consider a normal life. It is sad to say, but many of the ones I know have broken marriages, and it is the man – the husband – who has left because he can't, or won't or doesn't want to be part of a "difficult" child's life. Embarrassment was a word the adoption manager used; a lot of parents, both men and women, feel embarrassed being seen with a child with disabilities.

My heart goes out to all the parents who continue to love and bring up their children under these conditions. There must be so much love out there.

So most, if not all, of the children in care and waiting to be adopted have some kind of mental turmoil going round and round in their little heads. It seems that the government authorities really try hard to keep families together, even in cases involving abuse. They try to reason with the parents, suggest classes to improve their lifestyles, enrol them on courses to resolve their anger or addiction issues. The sentence used far too often is "Children are better off being with their natural parents". At what point does the system kick in and say enough is enough.

She reminded me of the tragic story of Baby P, the seventeen-month-old English boy, who had died in 2007 after having suffered more than fifty injuries over an eight-month period. He had been seen repeatedly by Haringey Children's Services and several NHS professionals. He should have been taken away from his parents long before his tragic death. The system had been too late in intervening. I told her I did remember the tragic story; it had been so sad. Then I asked her, "Baby P was repeatedly seen by whom?" She replied, "Haringey Children's Services – and other services, I'd imagine." I knew I recognised the name. My mother and baby home had been run by Haringey Children's Services – or perhaps it had been called Haringey Council at the time. Anyway, we glossed over that.

I remembered how, at the time, the story had shocked everybody, including the government. It certainly made them a lot more aware of how to deal with children in the care of violent, abusive parents. Many more children have come into the care system on the back of Baby P. In a lot of cases, the abused children are temporarily taken into care, while the parents try to sort themselves out. The children are then reunited at a later date, only to be abused and neglected again. The children are then passed from foster carer to foster carer, all the time reinforcing in their minds that they are living in an uncaring world. Don't get me wrong; most, if not all, foster carers are invaluable. They are caring people, who give a child a home and a share of their own family's life. However, a life without stability – just being passed around – obviously has its problems for the child. Without foster carers, where would these children be? Probably institutionalised in *Oliver*-type workhouses and mental-hospital-style prisons.

These days, the government is so desperate for new foster carers and people looking to adopt. Life without such people doesn't bear thinking about.

The government today is persistent in trying to reduce the number of children in care. But do they actually care about the children or are they worried about the numbers growing into an uncontrollable financial burden on the economy? Foster carers do get paid to look after the children. I am sure most foster carers don't do it for the money alone. It does cost a lot of money to bring up children. Is this the reason the government is desperate to reduce the numbers? Adoptive parents do not get any financial help whatsoever. I do agree the system has to be addressed in some way. That is why I am fully supportive of both foster carers and adoption, and I always will be.

The adoption manager told me there is no way we are going to stop, or even reduce, the number of unwanted or neglected children being born. She went on to say that some of the senior managers in her profession were looking to put a case forward, encouraging disabled parents (with physical or mental disabilities) to find out whether their unborn child has physical or mental issues, and, if so, to encourage them to have an abortion – offering support and financial assistance where necessary.

She really stressed how, with so many children out there in need of a mother, father, home and loving family, they need more people to come forward and adopt. I asked her how she and her colleagues went about looking for people. She said, "We use press adverts, TV adverts – campaign after campaign, looking for people to adopt, even large poster promotions on buses. There is a National Adoption Week in October/November. We always have a big campaign around that time. We're really getting desperate and the government is investing a lot of money promoting it. We also have a lot of open days, where people can come along and ask as many questions as they like."

I asked her if the government was setting targets and putting pressure on the adoption agencies to reduce the figures of children needing parents. She said she would rather not answer that question.

So my next question was about who can adopt – what type of person is suitable? She said, "Anyone really." I replied, "Okay, let's turn my question around. Who can't adopt?"

She explained that there are four categories of people who cannot adopt:

1. If you are under the age of twenty-one. There is no written rule about the upper age limit; however, offering a child to a frail elderly person would not be recommended.
2. If you do not have a legal right of residency in the UK. Non-residents of the UK are obliged to deal with the adoption authorities in their own country.
3. If you have been cautioned or guilty of offences against children.
4. If you are a smoker.

I was a bit shocked at the last one – and said so. I could understand the rest, but that last one would mean I would never be able to adopt a child. She replied, in a very abrupt manner, "No, Steve, you wouldn't be accepted. You should give up; it's bad for you." Does being a smoker really make you a bad parent – some would say yes. *Let's move on,* I thought.

She explained that, in the 1960s, the adoption agencies considered prospective adoptive parents as people who were married (which at that time implied they must be heterosexual), who had well-respected jobs, who owned a home or had the prospect of doing so soon, and who had Christian beliefs and would encourage the child to follow Christian worship. She continued, "Nowadays, anything goes: gay, lesbian, single people, any religious groups are welcome. But not a smoker; they're very firm about that." She gave me a hard look before going on, "Transsexuals, cross-dressers and transvestites – we'd have a look at all types of people these days. They're having a major push at the moment, looking for gay and lesbian couples. The reason is that, if they've been abused by a woman all their lives, some children feel more at ease with men. And it works the other way round; if they've been hurt or abused by men, they prefer the company of women. Our motto is Love is Enough."

I said, "There must be thousands of people out there wanting to adopt. There certainly was in the 1960s."

"No, not as many as you think. Medical advances and pregnancy-enhancing drugs and treatments these days help woman who can't have children. There was nothing around like that in your time. If your parents were living today, there would probably be some kind of operation or medicine to help. Plus, a lot of people don't want a troubled child."

My meeting with her was making me feel sad. I didn't show it – or maybe I did, but we carried on.

She continued, "There are more black children out there than white ones needing parents – not an issue for a lot of couples, but some couples say a white couple holding hands with a coloured child, and the other way round, is saying to everyone around you that this is not my blood child. I've been told it's like holding a big banner up with 'This isn't my real child!' written on it. How very sad and socially naïve in this changing multicultural world.

"Some people thinking of adoption as an option are being put off because they believe the system doesn't support them enough. They say there are so many hoops to jump through and thresholds that prevent you from adopting. Others say you're treated with so much suspicion and have to adhere to so many rules and regulations. There are also old stories flying around, such as you can't keep pets and a child mustn't share a room with another child. This simply isn't the case. The goal posts have moved so much and are continuing to do so these days. Yes, there are a lot of questions that we need to ask. Obviously, it's a big thing to take on, and it can have its difficulties. But we try to fit the right children with the right parents."

I asked her what sort of questions they asked. She told me to have a look at the Adoption UK website for the details, and then added, "Prospective parents are also required to have various meetings with experienced child psychologists. All this is very worthwhile and necessary because they'll probably be taking on a child with psychological scars of some kind and a history of abuse or neglect. They need all the help they can get. Bringing up a child in normal circumstances is hard enough. They'll be given on-going help and invited to lots of social events with people in the same situation as themselves."

"So, how are the children matched?" I asked.

"The couple will have had all the meetings and counselling. Once all the boxes have been ticked and they've been given the okay, we then agree to finding them a child. We give them Internet websites and brochures to look at – pages and pages of children's profiles and pictures. They're also invited to open days, where they can actually meet the children who are available."

I did find that hard to take in. It sounded a bit like catalogue retail shopping or bloody eBay. I didn't say that, but that was my first reaction. I could just imagine parents going to these open days and picking the pretty blonde-haired girl with pigtails, who was wearing a nice polka-dot dress, or the friendly faced boy who was sitting playing quietly with his cars, making engine noises. Meanwhile, all the troublesome ones would be sitting by themselves in the corner, desperately trying to get some attention by shouting, crying and throwing things. They don't get a look in. They are the left-over children who get to come along to the next special open day.

I was shown some of the online pictures and profiles. The profiles are always very positive. I guessed that, in some cases, they were probably a fragment of the truth. Let's take Johnny as a potential scenario. He has been abused by his parents so much that he hates people. He bites and is constantly spitting at people. He is an extremely naughty little boy. Now the adoption agency won't say that, but you're going to find out if you choose him.

Cynically, I can only relate this to buying a house, where the estate agent's claim of "nice sea views" means the frosted bathroom window faces the sea. His "large studio apartment" means it is a bedsit. "A liveable-sized lounge" means it's like a cupboard and a "comfortable-sized garden" means there is a small patio area.

I completely understand that the adoption agencies need to be positive and promote the good things. I just hadn't been aware of how it works these days; it reminded me of a retail shopping experience. I was completely taken aback when I found out.

The system also works the other way round. The child is given brochures and sites to look at with pictures and profiles of prospective adopters. She showed me a video while I was there. It brought me to tears again. It was of a little girl looking at a laptop, flicking through the screens saying, "I'm just looking on the website to see if anyone wants me."

I must stop being cynical. It's just that it was so different from how the adoption process worked when I'd been adopted, and it was really upsetting me. If this system works, that's great. It was all just a bit of a shock.

I suggested we broke for lunch. I was buying, so we left the office for an hour. We ended up in a nice Chinese restaurant just around the corner from her office. I think it was one of her favourites, as the owner greeted us with open arms and knew her name. We were given the best table and, before we had even sat down, a bottle of the best house red and two glasses were put in front of us. She was very interested in the fact that I was writing my adoption story. I had told her before I asked for a meeting. I got the impression she had never met an adult adoptee before.

She'd obviously spent a lot of her working life in social work offices and adoption agencies. I think the reason she'd agreed to having a private meeting with me was because she wanted to learn about the long-term mental affects from the other side – my side. She was also a jazz fan and had been to a few of my concerts after the wedding. We had kept in touch through social media.

I told her the subjects I was covering and the information I had discovered. She was interested in my foundlings story, and our conversation soon got round to feral children for some reason. She seemed to know a lot about it; I knew nothing. She thought it might be an interesting addition to my adoption story.

She explained that a feral child is a human child who has lived in isolation from human contact from a very young age. Such a child has no experience of human care, human loving, social behaviour or language. Most of them have severe intellectual or physical impairments, having been confined by their parents or guardians. "It's a bit like abandonment," she said. "You wouldn't believe it really happens, but there are lots of real cases of people who keep children locked up like animals – even children who were brought up by animals."

I really wasn't sure this was a subject I wanted to know about or write about, but she said she had met parents who treated their children like animals. Those children had been brought into her care system and later adopted.

She lightened the conversation by saying it appears in mythological and fictional stories. An example is the story of Mowgli from Rudyard Kipling's 1894 novel *The Jungle Book*. Mowgli is raised by wolves and becomes king of the jungle. In J.M. Barrie's book, *Peter Pan*, written in 1902, we read of the boy who fled to the magical world of Neverland and refused to grow up. The Penguin in the film *Batman Returns* spent his childhood amongst penguins in Gotham City's sewers. Then there is the famous story of Romulus and Remus, the main characters in the myth relating to the foundation of the city of Rome. Rhea Silvia, their mother, abandons her twins to die in the river. But they are found and cared for by animals in the forest, including a she-wolf and a woodpecker. Later, they are fostered by a shepherd and his wife.

I am glad she lifted our grim conversation, but she added, "If you're going to write a story about abandonment, you may as well mention the worst cases too."

We had finished lunch and had moved onto coffee, when she started to explain about another addition to the current adoption process, which I found so different from the way things were in the 1960s. These days, when receiving their adopted child, new adoptive parents are given a life-story book. This book gives details of the child's life so far. When we got back from lunch she showed me an example of a life-story book. My first reaction was one of shock; this was exactly the opposite of what happened in the 60s. Back then, the new parents were told nothing about the child and nothing about the parents, nor did they ever meet.

She told me the format of the book has been designed to help the adoptive parents start to share information with the child from an early age by introducing the idea of how families are different and how they are made up. In the book there are pictures and details of the child's blood family and relatives and foster carers who have looked after the child. There is a page letting the child know a bit about adoption; it explains that some children live with two dads or some children live with two mums – and all the variations.

One section read: "Sometimes children live with their birth families, who gave birth to them; sometimes children live with just one of their parents; sometimes children live with their grandparents or a relative; sometimes children live in different families from their brothers and sisters; sometimes children live with foster carers who take care of them; and sometimes children live with their forever family when they have been adopted."

Adoptive families are now known as forever families, which is a good positive name because it means being a family forever.

The life-story book is made up to help the child understand the concept of adoption and the journey the child has been on in order to reach the new forever family. It is designed to help adopted children know about their birth family, why they can't live with them and why they were taken away.

It goes on to say what the child has been good at – for example, music or sport – and some of the things the child has liked – for example, animals or painting – whilst staying with other people, including the birth parents and other blood relatives. The book goes into a lot of detail and provides useful information, especially for the new parents, who are trying to understand and deal with their new adopted child.

Then I turned to a page that shocked me. It read: "The purpose of this section of the book is to help the child's adoptive parents introduce the birth parents as soon as possible and explain why the child could not be cared for by their birth family."

Later in this section it said: "Life-story books are to be used, not stored in a cupboard, and introduced at a very early age. It is hoped that the child will have open access to their books." These words were underlined. It shows pictures of the birth family and mentions their names, where they live and went to school, their hobbies and achievements – it contains a lot of details. Then it goes into the reasons why the parents couldn't keep the child. The example I was looking at told the child that both parents had taken many drugs and were very heavy drinkers. It explained to the child that his parents would always end up in a big fight and continued, "You and your mummy often got very hurt and the police had to be called." They certainly don't flinch from being honest.

I had to stop reading there and put the book down. It just reinforced my views that things are so very different now.

I know I keep saying it, but adoptive parents in the 60s knew very little about the child's blood parents; I think it was the law at the time – no names, no family history, nothing. What you didn't know, you couldn't discuss. So, if the inquisitive adopted child were to ask their adoptive parents any questions, there would be no debate. You would just have to move onto another conversation. There was no dwelling on names, addresses, and no spending hours yearning and crying over old pictures. It was all about the future and moving on together. But at some stage we adoptees do want to know, and the new policy today is to be honest and reveal virtually everything – the good, the bad and the indifferent – at a very early age. This new book certainly is an eye opener and gives everybody a totally open policy.

I believe that having easy access to pictures of your blood parents at such a young age can have adverse effects. I was fifty when I decided to search. Why so late? I simply wasn't ready; I was neither mentally nor emotionally strong enough. Even at fifty years old, it is breaking my heart seeing the photos and discovering the information.

Take this scenario. Parents and children are constantly falling out over silly little things and, if the child has an emotional tool to upset and break their parents' hearts when they tell them off or they disagree with them, they will use it – such as remarking how their real mother wouldn't have done this or said that. If the adoptive father doesn't like sport or football, the adopted child can easily turn to his new dad and quote from the book saying that his real dad loved football and would have taken him to games and encouraged him to play. The children have the cards to play in arguments and the new parents don't know the rules and have never played the game. One up all the time for the kids.

I remember how I sometimes used to shout at my parents in anger, "You can't tell me off; you're not my real parents!" But that would be it. I had nothing else to throw at them. I had nothing to say about my blood parents because I didn't know anything about them.

With so much information available, you can't help but build up comparisons. They had a dog. Why don't you like dogs? My real mother had dark hair. Don't you like dark hair – why do you dye yours blonde? Little things, but it must be a constant threat. I don't think that children should have the upper hand – a master card up their sleeve, a blank scrabble piece they can use anywhere and at anytime they like.

The book talks about giving the child a family tree. How confusing is that, especially when asked to do it for a school project and show everybody. You put your hand up in class and ask the teacher, "Do you mean my real blood parents' tree or my adoptive parents' tree, miss?" Now everybody at school knows you're adopted. And I know how that feels. It isn't good – you get teased and bullied and you become an outsider.

If the book is kept in the child's room – let's say under the bed, as is suggested in one report – and the child is privately looking at it all the time, they may start thinking that the grass is greener elsewhere. We don't allow young children to take their laptop computers upstairs, but this could be worse. Dreams are also strange things. With this book you get to know so much about your past so early on that you could easily build up a fantasy story of how it was, how it could have been, how it still perhaps could be. It creates a huge yearning for missing blood sisters or brothers.

There is also one important thing I have missed. In the 1960s, most, if not all, adoptive parents changed the child's first name, and all of them changed the child's surname to their own. I don't think it's possible to do this with the new open-house policy. The children generally keep the name given to them by the people who had hurt them the most – a constant reminder for the new parents.

This is not always the case, as there seems to be different adoption options: closed adoption and open adoption – and varieties in between. The decision as to which option is followed is made by the courts and can be a bit confusing. Closed adoption is where there is no information about the birth family or the adoptive family made available to the other side. No information is shared and there is no contact between the families. After the adoption is finalised, the records are sealed, and the name of the child can be changed. Open adoption, on the other hand, allows for association and meetings with the birth parents. This can range from sharing photographs and letters, making phone calls and carrying out several authorised and supervised visits per year. In this case, the child's name would almost always remain the same, including the surname.

How can a new parent ever forget that (in most cases) the blood parents have hurt or abused their new bundle of joy? The name and the book is a constant reminder. The adoptive parents even have the blood parents' names. They could easily find them using the information in the life book and plan some sort of revenge. I'm not saying that would happen, but it is a thought. I've seen my son hurt really badly by a bigger boy playing football. I was watching on the touchline. He wasn't even anywhere near the ball and I had to just watch him crying his eyes out in pain rolling on the floor. I wasn't allowed to help him. It wasn't easy.

We moved our conversation onto open adoption. This is where the child has regular visits to see their blood parents. In a lot of cases the authorities insist on it, saying it is good for the child. I could see real problems for the new parents accepting this. The adoption manager said that you must think of the child first. I was a little confused about this one. She also went on to say the European government is really pushing for more open adoptions these days.

I know of an open adoption like this. Some people who live near me have this arrangement with their adopted children. They tell me that when the children go to see their blood parents – which is always supervised by one of them – the blood parents shower them with gifts. They are buying their affection, I suppose, but it does confuse the children; inevitably, they come back to their adoptive parents and their behaviour deteriorates, quite often becoming aggressive. I am told it takes them days, sometimes weeks, to get over it. I am also told they have to keep the original name and surname of their blood parents. This must be confusing as hell at school.

As I said, I am not sure about this new government rule of open adoption. Does it really help the kids? Possibly in some cases, but I see it as just another head fuck-up for the kids and three steps back for the new parents.

Having just looked back over my previous statements, I can see that I have been pretty scathing and unsupportive of this modern-day adoption process. I must try to see the positive aspects about the new life-story book and open adoption policy.

The world is a changing place and the governments of the day are pushing for a new transparency in adoption. Be open. Be truthful. Say it as it is. Let everyone know the facts and they can make up their own minds. Put all your cards on the table and play fair. Let the people decide. Or is it the child who decides?

Okay, you're given all the details as a child; there's no need for anything to be hidden. The truth is the best policy. It will make the child a stronger, more respectful person, who loves you more. Actually, I'm not sure. Yes, in the child's primary years, they may have a point. But when the child goes to secondary school, becomes a teenager and reaches puberty, I can see problems.

Sorry, I was trying to find positive things, wasn't I! I do think it is important for children to understand what has happened to them in life. For most children the birth parents can answer all the questions, show them pictures and provide details of every step of their lives. However, I have spoken to a few parents who have adopted children, and they believe this book is dangerous. One such parent said, " I don't want my child to read about what happened. It's scary. There's information in it that I never want my child to read." Another said it didn't give the true story of what had happened; it just glossed over the truth in a fairy-tale way.

Our meeting was getting heated. I could see that she, too, questioned the new system and was having to deal with problems thrown up by it on a daily basis. She agreed with me that the teenage years are the most testing for an adoptee. You're telling me! They are on their own a lot more, which means they have time to think. Children at that age can be very cruel. All they want to do in those years is be the same as their mates. With the vast amount of social networks available, children are choosing to spend long periods alone, staring at a screen, in deep thought. At the touch of a button they can see anything they want or go anywhere in their heads. They can also send messages anonymously. The new cyber-bullying generation is here.

Let's talk about Facebook for a moment. Today's adopted child now has access to this vast database of potential family members. He or she will have a life-story book, which provides the names and details of blood parents, sisters and brothers. At the touch of a button, they can easily trace blood relations and have secret relationships with them without the new parents ever finding out. The child could be sent friend requests by relatives and build up secret relationships with them. Also, if the new parents are on Facebook and put up pictures of their children, these pictures could easily be downloaded and added to the blood family's sites. In my opinion, the situation could quickly and easily escalate out of hand.

I'd had to be counselled, checked and vetted by my adoption manager, Sue, before being allowed to start my search. I'd had to get her permission to take the next step. And she had insisted that

I tell her all about my destructive years in Brighton. I am glad I had to go through that process. She helped me all the way and was there as a mediator if I needed it.

Some of my generation's adoptees say it was hell growing up, wondering where you came from and whom you look like. It was difficult for me, don't get me wrong; and it was confusing as hell sometimes. Those days are long gone; the new generation of adoptees is upon us – no secrets, no lies.

Let's all be open about everything? Sorry, I am a bit old-fashioned, I suppose. The coming generations may prove me wrong. I look forward to hearing and seeing how the new generation of adoptees grow up with this new open policy. I really hope it works for them.

Our meeting ended. It had been fascinating. I thanked her very much for her time and promised her I would send her a copy of my book when it is published.

Chapter 17

I had convinced myself I had spoken to Billie. This time I wanted to speak to Geoff. I now knew a lot about him. He sounded like a very talented, honest and caring person. I had made contact with members of his family, and they all spoke very highly of him.

The main question I wanted answered was whether he had told anyone about me.

My adoption rep, Sue, did not really approve of me going to see a medium. She didn't believe in such things but said that, if I was happy, then it was okay by her. My wife thought it was a stupid idea. She reminded me of how it had affected me the last time I had been; it had mucked my head up for days afterwards.

All the searching and information I had gathered along the way was a real head-spinner anyway, and I felt I had to keep going. Yes, I was drinking far too much. And, yes, I was smoking far too much. But I felt I was nearly at the end of my quest and, when I had finished, when I had answered all the questions, I would pull all my thoughts together, collect all my findings, gather up all the bottles of whisky hidden away and put them in a drawer and close it. But at the moment I was still climbing the mountain, still collecting pieces of my jigsaw.

The day came for my second session with my two old ladies and their friend. Was I looking forward to it? Yes, I suppose I was. I wasn't as anxious or as nervous as I had been before. I had already stepped into the unknown at my last meeting. I'd had a good look around and knew how to get out, so I thought a little poke around for a final time could be interesting.

I arrived early at Stella's house. We had a nice cup of tea; I had taken along a homemade cake. Stella, Connie and I have known each other for years. They love their jazz and are big fans of my band. Both of them take great comfort in spiritualism and have been dabbling in it for many years. Their husbands had both died, and they strongly believed they were in contact with them. Stella had been in contact with many lost relatives, and she claimed to be a stronger person for it. Connie is a real character – very strong willed and stubborn, and so sensitive to the other side of life it makes me laugh.

I felt at peace with them. They were people I could talk to about after-life experiences without having that look people give you – the one of misbelief, where they think you are crazy.

We discussed who would go first. The lady had not arrived yet, and each one of us would have some private time with her. Stella took me into her conservatory and showed me where we would have our meeting. She had laid a table with a crisp, white linen tablecloth and had put a notepad and pen next to a jug of water with two glasses. She said, "She does like to have a glass of water, you know." Also on the table was the legendary box of tissues. I knew what these were for now.

I joked with Stella and asked her if she had an egg timer. She laughed and said, "We're not at the church now. She'll give you as much time as she can." Stella had got to know this lady very well since my last visit. She had stayed the night at Stella's house on her previous visit. She told me a story about the lady. Apparently, even as a child, she'd had a talent for speaking to people from the other side, and she often got teased at school for having imaginary conversations in the playground. I bloody bet she did!

There was a knock at the door. I heard it from the garden, as I was out there having a cigarette. Stella called me in. She said, "You go first. She wants to get started straight away."

Stella took the lady's coat and led her through to the conservatory. Stella passed me a note pad and pen and told me to wait a few minutes before going in. As I mentioned before, I have chosen not to use the name of the lady in my writing.

I recognised the lady from last time. She was a pretty blonde – a small lady, very normal looking really. She was probably slightly older than me, but not by much.

I explained to her I had met her before. She said she recognised me from the church. I shook her hand and kissed her on the cheek. We both sat down. She said, "Please, feel free to make notes. I don't mind." I told her I had a good memory. The cynic in me was thinking that, if she saw me writing something down, she could use it in her reading and expand on it. Was I more sceptical than the last time? I tried not to be.

She closed her eyes for a few moments and clasped her hands together. I waited and watched, with Billie's main healing crystal in my hand – one of the ones from the box given to me by Penny. Then she began, "There are two people with us today. There is a lady coming through, but there is a man in the way, trying to stop her, telling her to be quiet. He is saying, 'This is rubbish. Don't speak to him. Leave him alone.' He is not happy." I asked who the man was. She said, "He says he is your father. He doesn't like this at all and is uncomfortable with me helping you." I asked her to carry on because I wanted to speak to him. She said, "I remember this lady from last time. I must ask her to calm down and let the man speak."

I could smell her perfume again and asked the medium if she could smell something. She said, "Yes, it's normal; spirits try to connect through the senses by sending lovely smells." Then continued, "These two people are so different. They are like chalk and cheese."

I stood up and put Billie's crystal on a shelf on the far side of the room, and then I sat back down. I thought it might calm her down and make her less receptive.

I asked her to concentrate on the man and to tell the lady present to leave.

The medium said, "The woman says she is your mother, Billie. Her language is terrible." I replied casually that I knew who she was, and that I would like to speak to the man.

Whatever I said or did made her go away. The medium said, "We have a man with us now. He knows all about you. He says he is very proud of the way you've turned out. He says he is very happy that you are writing a book about everything. Does that mean anything to you?"

I told her it did, and she continued, "Your writing is going to lead you to London sometime. I also see a film – not a feature film, something different. The lady is back. She's very strong willed. I can't ask her to leave again. She has powers – strong powers – and won't go." Then in a loud voice she said, "Just stand there and please be quite!" I was startled by her loud voice and started to feel a bit scared. She continued, "Writing your book is hurting you, isn't it?"

"Yes," I replied.

"You've not to worry. This lady says she'll be with you all the way. She'll help you, support you and guide you."

"Please tell both of them that I'm sorry that my searching was too late. Can I talk to the man? Can you tell me his name?"

"That might be difficult. I'll try, but they don't often tell me their names."

Suddenly, she grabbed hold of the table with both hands. Her whole body shook and her face began to sweat. "He says his name is Geoff. Does that mean anything to you?"

"Yes. Can I talk to him?"

"You can. He's still with us."

"I've spoken to your wife. I'm sorry, but I've told her about me and it's hurt her. She's really not happy."

Through the medium, he told me that he knew, and it was okay. He asked me to pass a message on to her, telling her that he loved her and that he would like to send her roses.

I continued, "Can I ask you another question? Did you ever tell anyone about me?"

The medium started to shake her head and told me that he'd said that he hadn't, even though it had been difficult not to. I asked why? The medium replied that it had been best that way, as he had never wanted his wife to find out. I said that I had just told her and the family too. He told me it was okay. I asked whether he had told his brother. He replied, "Nobody, not even Peter."

The medium continued, "Billie wants to talk to you again. She wants to help you in any way she can with promoting adoption and helping those poor children who are desperate for families, She wants you to make sure you do this in your writing." I said that I would.

"She also said she hopes your writing helps people understand adoption and that people who have been adopted lose their pain by our words. Then she said you know I am helping you write, Clive, don't you, dear?" I didn't know what to say. She went on, "Billie is happy you've moved her. She said she's happy up there as long as you are both in the same house. She doesn't want the two of you to be apart again. Does this mean anything to you?" I nodded.

She continued, "Billie has lots of energy, hasn't she? She's very strong and very spiritual. She's one of the strongest people I have met in the other world. I don't usually get their names. Is there anything more you'd like to ask?"

I probably had lots of things to ask but, to be honest, I was feeling uncomfortable and a bit scared by this stage. I just wanted to finish the meeting. Had I got what I wanted? Who knows?

I politely ended the meeting early. The medium said it was very nice to meet me again and repeated that she didn't very often get their names. It had only happened to her once before, so she told me she considered the lady to be a very special person. I thanked her, held her hand and kissed her on the cheek again. I left my money on the table and slowly walked out. I thanked Stella and Connie and said I would be in touch, and then I quickly made my way home.

The conversation was going around in my head. How did she know his name, or Billie's name again, or Geoff's brother's name, or my first name, or that Billie had spiritual powers? How did she know I was writing a story, or that I'd moved Billie's ashes into the loft, or that I'd been adopted? After our meeting, I confirmed that I was writing a book and asker her if I she would mind whether I included the details of my visits to her. She was happy for me to do so.

If this medium was for real, and I had talked to Geoff, I had just found out he hadn't said anything to anybody about me, which was a shame. I don't know how Geoff could have kept me a secret all his life. He was very close to his jazz musician brother, Peter, in Australia. Rose had told me so, and there are many pictures of them together with large glasses of whisky in their hands. You would have thought after a heavy drinking session he might have said something.

I do think mediums have their place. I think they are clever, very intuitive and have a higher sense of perception than most people. But, come on, they are playing a game with our minds. I had been willing to play the game – but only for that half-hour before in the church and another half-hour today. My wife was right; this was mucking up my head again. This time I was even more confused; I felt empty inside, and I also felt sick.

That afternoon, I came home and decided to get in contact with the girl I'd met at Billie's funeral in Brighton. She had told me Billie had been a spiritualist and a spiritual healer. She's also mentioned to me that Billie might get in contact with me one day. She'd given me her card on the day of the funeral, asking me to keep in touch. Her name was Maria. I wondered if she would be able to make any sense out of all this spiritualist, afterlife stuff.

I emailed her that evening, telling her my story so far. I explained that I was confused about my experiences with the medium and that I'd started to write a book about it all. I asked her whether she wanted to contribute her thoughts. Very soon, I got a reply from Maria with a few words for the book:

Billie was a lovely friend whom I met in the latter part of her life through our mutual friend Penny. I used to visit her on many afternoons, and we spent hours talking about life and spirituality. Billie was a healer for many years and worked at the local hospital, offering healing to those in need. She was even presented with an award by the hospital for the healing services she had given, and she was very proud of this fact. I myself am a spiritual healer and have been practising for a number of years with both people and animals. I used to do healing on her beloved cat, Jack. Billie and I loved nothing more than chatting about the world beyond our realm.

Billie often spoke about the son she'd had to have adopted and hoped that he knew how much she loved him and that she had not wanted to give him up. But she said that, in those days, she was just not allowed to keep him because of the social stigma. She said that she treasured the little time she'd had with him before he was taken and had told him how much she loved him. She even said that she wrote him a letter explaining her feelings. Billie never forgot him and had always hoped that he would try to find her, so it was very bitter–sweet that Steve just missed her passing by about a year as I know she would have loved to have met him. However, knowing Billie, the strange occurrences that have happened since Steve has had her ashes are no surprise to me. She'll do all she can to make contact with him from the other side. She will not want to be left out from making contact with him now that he has found her friends who loved her. I have often felt her presence around and have felt blessed that she has come through to me after her passing. I often see lights flashing on and off and feel her very strong energy around me, particularly when Penny comes over to spend an evening at my flat. Billie is simply letting us know that she is around. It is no surprise to me that she would want to make her presence known. It is very common for spirits to use their energy to try to affect things physically, particularly around a home. They try to let their loved ones know that they are present and want to make contact with them. I am so pleased that Steve visited the medium as it sounds like she was so accurate. It is not always easy for mediums to get the names of people so, for me, this is a clear indication that Billie and Geoff were present and making sure that they made contact with Steve and got clear messages to him. I hope this gave Steve some comfort; the fact that he became emotional tells me that there was a strong energetic connection made between the two worlds.

Billie was a very forthright person and had a great sense of humour. We shared a lot of laughter, and she was always there with sound advice for me. I have often called upon her assistance from above when I am carrying out healing work, as I know how powerful she is, even from the other side. I was lucky enough to be with her in her final days at the hospital and gave her healing to comfort her as she prepared to pass over. We tried to keep her appearance as immaculate as possible; she had always loved to look her best and wear her make-up. We were particularly fortunate as one of her friend's, Jay, was working as an auxiliary nurse at the time, and he took such great care of her by tending to her needs outside his working hours. He made sure she was as comfortable as possible and that her appearance was kept as she would have wanted it.

Billie would be thrilled to know that Steve is writing a book about his journey to find her; she had loved to be in the limelight when she was younger. Billie had been a model and had shown me very beautiful photographs of her in her glamorous modelling days. When she was married to Teddy, she lived in a beautiful home, and it was even featured in the Town and Country magazine. When I met Steve I could see the resemblance to Billie immediately, and the fact that he was a musician and flamboyant character made so much sense, knowing Billie. I think this book will enable Billie's memory to *live on through Steve and, hopefully, comfort those who have lost loved ones – or those who have not been able to locate their loved ones in this life, as there is life beyond this world.*

Thank you, Maria, for those touching words. She seemed to confirm Billie's talent for spiritualism and backed up a lot of what I had found out about her.

I remembered that Billie had been involved in some miracle cures through her spiritual healing work, and I was keen to find out more about these. I asked Maria and Penny about them to see what they knew.

Penny sent me some information:

Dear Steve,

I only know a little about the miracle cures that Billie spoke of. One was someone with a spinal condition that caused her a great deal of joint pain. Billie said that she came to see her several times and, although the condition itself could not be cured, her pain was reduced to the point she could resume the life that had been put on hold due to pain and immobility. This happened before I knew her.

The other one that springs to mind (but I'm not sure if this was the second one as I think she may have had another when she was training to be a healer before I knew her) was a young man with a really bad skin complaint that no tablets or cream had been able to sort. He saw her about twice and it cleared up completely. I know that it would flare up occasionally and he would come to see her again and it would go. He chose to see her rather than have meds for it as it was so successful.

Love Penny x

Maria also wrote back to me:

Dear Steve,

As a healer myself, I know of the powerful effects it can have, both physically and emotionally. Healing is a way of channelling spiritual energy through the hands to another person or living thing, whether present or not. It can be sent over a distance as the energy is purely given by intention. The healer is a conductor of the energy and transfers it to the other person. It helps in times of trauma, life transitions and for personal and spiritual growth.

The field of Quantum Physics is fast becoming a more understood and recognised science. The universe, earth and all living things are made up of energy vibrations. As a healer you can affect these vibrations by channelling the chi energy (this is known as universal energy or vital life force) to rebalance and bring about homeostasis to the energy field of any living thing and allow its own natural healing abilities to increase in times of disease.

I also work with support and guidance from the spiritual realms, and the energy that comes through can vary in intensity depending on its source. Most of all, it is about the intention of love. The feeling of the energy as we experience it can be truly beautiful and relaxing. The more we grow spiritually, the more often we can experience how the healing energy feels. However, the healing energy works no matter what your level of spiritual development is or how much you feel. It goes where it needs to go and does what it needs to do.

Billie demonstrated the power of healing throughout her career and was highly recognised for her work. I was very privileged to know her and learn from her expertise.

Love Maria xxx

One of the things I was keen to have confirmed was whether Geoff had told anyone about me, so I decided to ask Peter's daughters, Rose and Jeanette, in Australia. I had been keeping in contact with both of them and was sure that, were they to know anything, they would tell me. They replied:

Hi Steve,

From what my mum told me, Geoff was going through a really hard time with Jayne after losing their daughter, who was only three. Jayne blamed him, even though it has now been confirmed that both parents need to carry the gene that causes cystic fibrosis.

Geoff was so sad, and that is when he turned to your biological mum for comfort and support. I do believe that my dad was his confidant and knew of you. He made out he was surprised when we first had contact, but I think he was delighted that you had found us.

Jeanette xx

Hi Steve,

All is well down this end of the world. Hope things are great with you.

As far as Dad knowing about you, I don't think he did, but he did tell me that he knew Geoff was troubled and had a secret that he was holding onto. After he learned about you, he said to Mum, "That explains a lot to me about my brother." Geoff loved kids and devoted his life to helping disabled children – maybe also to fill the gap of not being able to raise you. It must also have been hard for him living and dying with such a huge secret. He wanted to adopt a baby, but Jayne would not hear of it. He would have made a great dad.

Rose x

Thank you, Rose and Jeanette. It has been a privilege to get to know you. Both of you have been so genuinely welcoming throughout my difficult time searching.

So, conflicting views. I really don't think Geoff said anything to anyone. I suppose, it was just the way that generation did things in the 1960s – they kept secrets and just moved on with the times. He may even have used his feelings of guilt as motivation to help the many hundreds of children suffering from cerebral palsy. Also, if Geoff had said anything to anyone when he was alive, and Jayne had found out, it probably would have been the end of a long and very loving relationship.

Chapter 18

I have been keeping in regular contact with all my newfound family and friends. They are the link to my previously unknown past. I have also been keeping my real family in the loop with all my findings by telephone. I now feel closer to them than I have ever felt. Over the last few months, all my time has been spent selfishly researching and chasing lost, forgotten dreams. I hadn't been home to see them for ages. It was time to go and visit the family that I cared about most – the people who chose me, looked after me and gave me a fabulous upbringing.

It was great to see Mum and Dad again. During the phone calls to them, I had thought that they were okay about me searching. But now, seeing them face-to-face, I could see they had been hurt.

I had been telling Mum all my news on the phone, as I'd been discovering it. Dad was always in the background, wise and wonderful. Mum would have told him everything, but he never really made comments about it to me. Mum was always the one I gave my news to about most things. Dad was always there and listening. But he was frail and not very well; the years were catching up with him.

I bounced in the door, as I always did, and, after a family meal, I started talking to Mum about my adventures. I showed her the dusty old court files and legal documents I had received. I am not sure what kind of response I was expecting. I was excited and proud of my findings. Normally, Mum and I would sit up, into the early hours, chatting and putting the world to right. Not this night though. I wanted to show her all the files and letters I had found that told me who I was. She read all the paperwork with tears in her eyes. She was happy for me but didn't understand why I needed to look so far into my past. Had I not been loved enough? Had they not brought me up the way I had wanted? What had they missed? Had they done something wrong? Why was I trying to hurt them? "You've always wanted more," she said.

I showed her all the pictures I had, including the one of me in the arms of Billie at Red Gables, which had been taken by Geoff. What was I doing? Did I really expect her to be overjoyed by that – seeing her little baby boy in the arms of another woman?

The file was full of confidential documents relating to the adoption, letters sent to them years ago about me and notes from the adoption agency and the children's officers. Whilst I was portraying the sadness that Billie and Geoff had felt, she reminded me that it was one of the happiest times of her life. Billie's overwhelming sadness, pain and loss was my parents' gain. I was reminded about the happy times we'd had together and how overjoyed and excited they'd been the day they picked me up from the agency.

I told my mum that I was writing a story about it all. Like a paparazzi photographer or an over-keen journalist, I was still looking for more copy, more words, more answers.

I started to ask her about dates and her memories of the court case. Did you ever meet Billie? Did you ever meet Geoff? Did you ever go to Red Gables? How much information did you have about me? And then the bombshell question: why couldn't you have children? And I was on a roll. Was it you or Dad who had the problem? How did it feel not being able to have children?

I was sure she took offence at these questions, especially that last one. "It's personal," she said. "Neither of us could have children. I don't want you to write anything about me in your story." I went on to tell her I had met new cousins and had a huge new family tree. Did I really think she wanted to know these things?

When I told her I had spoken to Billie and Geoff, her face changed to utter disbelief. "What do you mean you've spoken to them?" I explained how I had hired a top medium and been to a spiritualist church. She told me not to be so stupid and completely disbelieved me. She told me that if I mentioned that in my story, people would think I'm a real nutcase. I wanted her to share in my findings; she had shared everything else in my life.

She asked why I was writing a story about it and whether I really wanted people to know my personal information. She wondered what my children will think if they read it. I said I thought it was an interesting story and asked her to help me with it. She was a writer; I had a story. She blankly refused, saying she wanted no part in it.

Originally, I had started to write my story thinking she would help me with it – help with my grammar, my spelling and my sentence structure. I have never read a complete book from cover to cover in my life. I just can't sit down long enough. How was I expecting to write one? Yes, I do read, but usually articles – and nothing over three thousand words. If I have to read anything longer, I just scan it. If I ever want to learn something, I preferred to watch a video or listen to audio instructions. I suppose, being a musician, I feel comfortable with sound not words.

If my mother wasn't going to help me with it, how was I expecting to write a book? She really wanted no part in it – and still doesn't, which is a shame as, otherwise, we could have heard her stories about my adoption. I started to worry that I wouldn't be able to do it, but I was determined to give it a go.

My sister came round the following day. I tried to get her interested. I thought she would be because she was also adopted. I showed her pictures and briefly told her my story. She listened, but I could see the disgust on her face. Mum had told her I was searching, so she probably knew most of my findings already. I don't think she felt comfortable hearing anything about it. She may have been jealous about me knowing so much. She could see I was confident in my belief that I'd spoken to Billie and Geoff and that I'd had the opportunity to thank them for my adoption. I also knew for certain that my blood mother loved me very much and never forgot me and always hoped I would get in touch – something an adoptee always wants to know.

I showed her a picture of Jennifer, Geoff's daughter, and stupidly I said she would have been my half-sister. I think she took offence to that too – understandably so; after all, she is my true sister.

I think that, over the past few months, as I'd been telling Mum everything on the phone, Mum had then been telling my sister. I assume they'd both been sitting round the table in disbelief and utter disgust about what I was doing. My sister would have realised how much it was hurting Mum, hearing all my news.

My sister wasn't happy with me at all, and I don't think she ever will be. There has always been an amazing amount of jealousy and rivalry between us – most of it, if not all, on my part. As a young child growing up, I was always asking my parents which one of us they loved the most. I don't think I was a very good big brother to her because of this; I was too interested in me. I was the one who was outwardly affected by my adoption. I allowed my feelings and frustrations to be seen by the family. I behaved badly and got upset by the smallest of things. I was the one who was constantly seeking out every ounce of their love and demanding their undivided attention.

The funny thing was, though, the following day, Mum told me that my sister had started to search. She had discovered that both her blood parents were from Australia. I knew it would be difficult for her to find any other information about them as they lived so far away – but not impossible, though. I don't think she wanted to know anymore anyway.

So, my findings had gained me new distant relatives – and a new distant family – and had answered a load of my questions. But in the process, I had lost my true sister's love and respect. I'm not sure whether that was due to the fact that I was searching for new family members or whether it was because I was being my usual self: her opinionated, arrogant, self-centred, overbearing big bad brother.

I headed home again, and, the following weekend, Penny and Chris came over. They had already been to stay with us on a few occasions, and we had build up a great relationship. We had a strong, natural bonding through Billie; Penny had been her best friend and I was her son. My true sister probably will not like me saying this, but, if I'm honest, Penny is like a new sister to me – an additional sister. We are the same age, which is nice. We were not raised together, but we do fit together in a strange way. Penny knew I was writing my story, and I asked her if she would say a few more words. She wrote:

I arrived home to find Chris waiting for me full of anticipation. He showed me a letter that had arrived from the company that had organised Billie's funeral. Enclosed was an email from a person named Steve, who stated he was Billie's son and was trying to trace information about his mother. He had contacted many of the funeral directors in Brighton as he had a copy of a death certificate showing Billie had died there. Obviously, the funeral director did not want to divulge my details, so they sent the communication on to me so I could decide what to do.

By that afternoon I was talking to Billie's son! Within days we had met and I have since visited him and his family in his hometown. This is so wonderful; I find it hard to put into words. I am so sad that Billie and he did not meet – they are like two peas in a pod! He is very like her to look at, although he has his father's dark hair and skin tone (I've now seen a photo of him that Steve has) and, having met several times, I'm afraid to say (sorry Steve!) their temperaments are very similar. I think Steve was worried that his mother was one of those "over-the-top" loud eccentrics because, as I said earlier, it is very difficult to describe Billie without making her sound that way. But Steve has the same way of dressing and carrying himself as his mother, which means he stands out from the crowd without the need to deliberately draw attention to himself. Another case of "once seen never forgotten"! I am still amazed by the fact that I have become the link between Billie and her son. Steve and his lovely family feel like my own, and I hope we can stay in touch for many years.

Touching words, Penny. Thank you. I take strength from having met you and from knowing you and your family so well. I also feel the warmth in our new sister–brother relationship. There is something very comforting in being around others who have been adopted; they really know how it feels.

Lesley and her husband have also been over a few times – not as formally as the first time but as friends. They were still delightful and very welcoming towards me. We have got to know each other reasonably well. We'll never be as close as regular family members, but I don't think that's how we'd want it anyway. Unfortunately, Jayne is still very upset about Geoff not telling her about me, but I've been told she is slowly coming to terms with it.

I explained to Lesley I had been back to see my medium lady again, and that I had spoken to Geoff. It was a personal thing, so I didn't expect her to understand or believe me. I told her about the message that Geoff had asked me to pass on: "Tell Jayne I love her and want to send her roses." Lesley had relayed the message to Jayne and, apparently, it had meant something to her, as roses were her favourite flowers and Geoff used to give her roses all the time. Anyway, I had done what Geoff had asked of me; I had passed the message on. I hoped it had given Jayne some comfort.

A couple of days later I received a message from Lesley saying a few of my other new cousins wanted to meet me. She warned me they were very cynical about me having just popped up out of the blue. They didn't believe my story; they wondered what I was up to. She also told me they were sisters and that one of them lived quite near me.

I welcomed the idea, of course, and said I was happy to meet them; I had nothing to hide. We all met up in my village at a local coffee shop. I felt as if I were on trial – a bit like the first time I'd met Lesley. This time, it was even worse. It felt as if I was in a courtroom. I was the innocent party and had done nothing wrong – no lawyer present, just me against the sisters. I had hurt a member of their family by giving Geoff's wife the news. They were angry. Was I after her money? Was I after the family jewels?

I told them briefly about the reason for my search and mentioned some of the information I had found out about Geoff. I had taken along the paperwork from the court with all Geoff's details on it to show them, as I had done when I'd first met Lesley. The paperwork was my witness. They kept asking if I was sure I'd got my story right. I think after the second cup of coffee, they started to believe me. They could see that all my searching was hurting me and that I was genuine. We started to talk about ourselves and exchanged pictures on our phones of our families. They began to realise that I wasn't making it up. We left it that we would keep in contact and might see each other again at some future family gathering.

I didn't like that side of my searching – not being believed, not being trusted, being silently accused of doing it for personal gain and financial wealth. The sisters never said those things, but I could see it in their eyes when we first met.

What they didn't realise was that I, too, could have been vulnerable throughout this reunion. If Geoff had still been alive, I would have been the one to look after him. Let's say he was in a lot of debt or had fallen on hard times; I would have been the one who would help financially or support him in some other way. I had already thought of this whilst I was searching. Things may have turned our very differently. It doesn't always turn out the way the TV adoption programmes portray it.

One of the sisters lives nearby, and we have met a few times. She is very pleasant. She really looks like a Boyce. She was interested in getting to know me better. It's funny really as she does a lot of charity work and is often in my local paper handing over cheques from her fundraising achievements, and I am in the paper with write-ups about my gigs and concerts. Indirectly we had both heard of each other.

A few months after our meeting, I had a call from Debbie, my new local cousin, to tell me that her husband had died. She wondered if I would go to the funeral to help support her. A lot of her family were invited. The service was going to be held in a local church, near where I live. I said I would be pleased to go.

My desire to search for my blood parents had begun at my wife's mother's funeral when I thought that no one in the world looked like me. This had affected me deeply. I had just been invited to my first blood-family funeral. Was it possible that I'd be able to look around the church and see people who looked just like me?

I parked the car in the cemetery car park to awaiting eyes. I could hear their silent whispers. Was he going to turn up? Who is this new member of our family we have heard so much about? I walked hesitantly over to the mass of people standing outside the church. Lesley and her husband greeted me with a hug and briefly introduced me to my relatives from the Boyce family.

I felt a little like a goldfish in a bowl. I was being watched by many people. It was obvious by now that I was who I said I was. There was no doubt that I was Geoff's son and a Boyce. I had nothing to prove on that day; my face was my passport and proof of who I was. It wasn't the best occasion to meet new blood relatives.

We all went into the church. Lesley took my arm, as she could see I was nervous. I knew the church well; I had been there many times before. My band has been asked to play in the church at funerals many times, and I have also attended lots of my friend's funerals there.

I wasn't playing on this day, but the spotlight was still on me. Between readings and hymns, I could see the heads turn. "That's him over there. That's Geoff's son." Lesley kept a tight grip of my arm. She knew people would be interested to see what I looked like. The service was emotional. I got to hear more stories about the Boyce family: their family occasions, their holidays and, of course, the sad story of Debbie's husband.

I enjoyed being there – if you can enjoy being at a funeral. I felt a bit of an outsider, but I knew I had every right to be there to support Debbie. I also thought that I was, in some strange way, adding a little bit of light to what was a sad occasion.

After a moving service, we were led out of the church, where we walked in a line, reading the messages on the flowers. I put my sunglasses on, but Lesley quickly asked me to take them off. "Let people see your face. You're part of the family now." She introduced me to many people – this is Steve, Geoff's son; this is your cousin x and your niece y. I am terrible at remembering names. I just smiled and made casual conversation.

I was asked if I would like to go back to the wake for refreshments. I hadn't planned to go but, on the day, I felt I should. I was also told that some of the relatives were hoping I would be there and wanted to meet me.

The room was filled with Boyces. At last, I was in a room with people who all looked vaguely like me. We all shared the same genes. Did it make us one big family? Did I feel more at peace with myself than I had done at my wife's mother's funeral? No, of course I didn't. I felt that I'd become two separate people, as if I were living a double life. It was bloody strange, bloody complicated.

The atmosphere always changes at a wake. The sadness and tears are left at the church and a more reflective celebration of life is put on the table, usually helped by a glass of something strong.

I didn't drink that afternoon as I had the car, but I was welcomed into the family in a very special way. Relatives came

214

up to me and introduced themselves in an informal, affectionate and sometimes emotional way. They told me stories about my blood father. All of them – I am very pleased to say – had wonderful memories and spoke very highly of him. I did feel proud on that day to be Geoff's son. I was representing Geoff for the first time; I was his only living child and carried his genes.

Jayne, Geoff's wife, wasn't there as she was too frail to travel. I would have liked to have met her but, on reflection, a family funeral probably wasn't the best place to meet for the first time.

I met lots of cousins and their children, one of whom looks remarkably like me in my younger days. He is also a musician, who lives in London. We had lots to talk about that afternoon. We had so much in common – well, about the music business, anyway. He was too young to think that I was a great new relative that he ought to get to know.

We all had a good afternoon. As they say, most families only ever meet together at weddings and funerals. We agreed we would all keep in contact. They made me feel very welcome that day. I thanked them for that.

I would like to meet Jayne one day; however, she is elderly and frail, and I don't think it will ever happen, which is a shame. She has had various opportunities to travel with Lesley when she has come to see me. I don't think she wants to meet me, and I can understand it from her side. She has seen many photographs of me; I do look like Geoff and that may upset her. Also, seeing my children might remind her of Geoff; my eldest son does look very like me. We keep in contact and my thoughts and stories are passed onto her through Lesley. I am so sorry I hurt her with my news. She didn't deserve it – neither of us did; we were both the innocent parties. I will never forget the day I told her.

I hope that one day I'll get to meet them all again. Perhaps next time I'll be invited to one of their big family weddings.

Chapter 19

I think there is a turning point in most adoptees' lives that forces them to either think about or start to take action regarding their adoption and the secrecy around it. It could be starting their search, seeking therapy or looking for some kind of healing process. There is usually some kind of trigger point. For me it was the birth of my first child, and this was then fuelled by my anxiety being at my wife's mother's funeral.

It seems we all share the same pain and confusion growing up. When a person is born into their biological family, there are hundreds of little genetic connections that may never be really noticed because they have always been there. Adoptees have none of these, but we do notice them in others – and I think we are affected in some way when we see them in others. I know I am.

I have been in contact with many adoption sites and forums on social media, and it has been refreshing and reassuring to hear from other adoptees and read other people's stories. It has made me realise that I am not the only person having a hard time, trying to work out who I was and wondering where I came from. Sharing is a great healing process. There are many sites out there, and they are reasonably easy to find. I put the word adoption into the top bar (search for people, places and things) on Facebook and found many that suited me.

Today we know that separation is traumatic for both the mother and the child; it affects the brain structure of those involved in the trauma. I don't think this was recognised back in the 1960s. We were the ones who had no choice; we just had to try to put all the broken pieces back together. I wish society would recognise the effect this has had on us, on our ability – or inability, rather – to heal. They seem to have a finger in every other aspect of adoption these days apart from the healing – no one wants to talk about that.

As a child I did attend therapy, but adoption healing was never mentioned. I would just play with shapes, build things out of blocks and draw pictures of animals. Dr O'Keeffe constantly told me to stop looking for water in a dry well. What the bloody hell was that all about? Was I being told to stop thinking about things so much?

I was suffering from genetic bewilderment. I felt disconnected from society. I was growing up wondering who I was and whom I looked like. At times, I felt that my parents and closest family members were strangers. I went through a phase of being very angry at the world and at myself, and it has been nice to know that I wasn't the only one who went through it. Mine wasn't the typical teenage identity rebellion; being adopted really mucked up my head for years – and still does a bit. I must have been very difficult to live with in my early years. In fact, I must be a little difficult to live with now as the adoption scars are still there. My parents have been my rock, my therapists and my punch bag. "You can't tell me off; you're not my real parents!" – what a thing to have shouted at you. I am sorry.

I know it may sound dramatic, but we adoptees feel as if we were abandoned at birth – second-hand, second-choice people, living with a sense of never really belonging anywhere, living a life of insecure transience. This feeling is just something we live with. People expect us to feel thankful and grateful; we are constantly told we are chosen, special and lucky. These words never make us feel any better. Just because we appear to be happy doesn't mean that deep down our hearts aren't broken. There are triggers I've had to learn to manage. Sometimes I do it well; sometimes I do it poorly.

All adoptees have issues growing up. I remember I used to cry constantly because I hadn't come out of my mummy's tummy and all my friends around me had. My mum told me that I had not grown in her tummy but, instead, in her heart. I worried that I wouldn't be able to live up to the expectations of the family who had adopted me. I hated the secrecy that went along with being adopted. A family isn't always about blood; it's about having the people in our lives who want us in theirs – the ones who accept us for who we are and who do everything to make us happy and cause us to smile. They love us, no matter what.

Most adoptees talk about grieving – grieving the loss of their blood parents. This was never addressed by our new families; they were just so happy to have us, and we had to hold back all the feelings and just stumble through them. Just because we hadn't grow up with our biological families, it didn't mean we didn't recognise it as a loss – one that very much affected us. The hurt doesn't just affect us growing up; we have to live with it all our lives.

Don't get me wrong; my parents were excellent. It was me who didn't want to discuss grieving or feeling hurt or confused in any way. I wanted to appear strong; I wanted to be strong. I didn't want them to get hurt or over concerned due to my insecurities.

My turning point was planning my search. I'd had enough of the disillusionment and uncertainty about who I was. I don't think anyone really noticed the huge bag of chips that I carried around on my shoulder for years. I had become a good actor, a good liar, developed the art of being sneaky. I'd had years of practice: hiding the past, avoiding questions, diverting situations and covering up my vulnerability. I'd just tried to live according to me dream and had hoped that things would work out. And I believe that having been a musician all my life has allowed me to live out my dream. If people love my music, I am happy. Standing on stage you can be anybody you want to be, and hearing the roar from a crowd and loud applause helps heal the wounds of anyone's pain.

I am not the sort of person who is constantly angry with the world – a huge number of adoptees are, and I completely understand why this is. They feel let down by their lack of identity, lack of origin. They feel helpless, like an outsider. Although I, too, have felt like this for many years, I am actually the complete opposite now. I am over sensitive and easily hurt by things such as homelessness, people with mental health issues, parents splitting up and, of course, my old chestnut, babies and children being brought up with no dads or by single parents. I suppose I have problems dealing with couples splitting up or hearing of extra-marital affairs because that's how it all started with me.

What really hurts me more than anyone will ever realise is the situation where my children argue with me, treat me as if I am useless or offload their anger onto me. Don't get me wrong; I am far from being the perfect dad; I am probably still carrying the selfish, self-centred, self-opinionated, attention-seeking banner around with me. I know it's just teenagers being teenagers, but it really hurts big time. Whenever we have verbal confrontations, I end up feeling so low and helpless inside. I have always wanted to be liked, and when I don't feel liked – or feel hated at times – it is so difficult to take. Of course, children disrespecting their parents is something that happens all the time, but I think that when you are an adoptee, living a rejected life as a second-hand kid, it hurts even more.

Discovering that the children coming into today's adoption system have been abused and neglected has made me incredibly sad. What gives me strength, however, is knowing that there are many caring people out there who want to adopt a child – the problem is that the government and the courts are constantly changing the goal posts. I find it really hard to keep up with the legislation. One minute the government is promoting adoption, and then the European courts change the rules. It confuses the hell out of me; it must also confuse the hell out of the professionals in the industry. I am not sure who knows what is best for the child.

I know that I am not unique. I went through what most adopted kids go through: feeling like an outsider, constantly searching for my identity, feeling sorry for myself and living with my lack of generic origin. The hurt caused by discrimination and bullying during my primary-school days took its toll. The kids at my school knew I was adopted and would tell me that their parents had said that my real mother didn't love me and didn't want me. Then, there's the one that all adoptees go through: lack of medical generic records – a constant reminder by health professionals that we are from another planet.

I have been lucky, I suppose. I found out where I came from. I now have lots of information about my blood parents. I know I was loved and missed. I know the reason for my adoption – so, now I ought to be happy, having had all my questions answered. I will always live with an element of pain, as it never goes away, but I now feel an internal peace. We adoptees need to be survivors; it is not always easy, but we all must try.

In getting to this point, my journey has been emotionally draining. I've hurt myself, and I've hurt others. At the start, I thought I could handle the journey. It was a huge gamble at the time; it could have turned out quite different, which would have completely turned my world upside down. I think many adoptees like to gamble and hurt themselves – I know I do.

I think one of the biggest things I have learned is that a huge number of adoptees feel the same way as I did growing up – and as I feel now. I take comfort in the fact that I am not alone in having those feelings.

If you are an adoptee reading this, I hope that you will understand that we are all in this together; we are all a team; we all support each other. You will never hear a bad word from an adoptee about another adoptee. It doesn't matter how bad they are or what they have done. We all have a special and unique understanding of each other. We are our own religion; we are our own species. I was reminded by a fellow adoptee recently of a few quotes from A.A. Milne's book *Winnie-the-Pooh*:

"If ever there is a tomorrow when we are not together ... there is something you must always remember. You are braver than you believe, stronger than you seem, and smarter than you think. But the most important thing is, even if we're apart ... I'll always be with you."

"I think we dream so we don't have to be apart for so long. If we're in each other's dreams, we can be together all the time."

So, what can I pass on from my experience? The search can be a difficult journey but, if you have spent your whole life wondering about it, you need to find out what has been troubling you. Just getting your original birth certificate and knowing your blood parents' names may be enough. You may want to see pictures. You may want to try to make contact and have a reunion. I have come to the conclusion that a family is not always defined by our genes; it is built and maintained through love.

If, like me, you were adopted in the 1960s, you may find your blood parents are already dead. I sought comfort and was advised to visit a spiritualist church. Previously, I would never have dreamed of doing that, and I don't want people to think I recommend it; it was just something I did for myself – my biological mother, Billie, was a spiritualist, so naturally I decided to go down that route. My little old ladies, Stella and Connie, who recommended this to me, are still around, although they are now frail and in ill health. They still come to my jazz concerts quite regularly. I keep in contact with them to this day.

As I've said many times, having a mentor – someone to guide and help you through the process – really helps. If you are hoping for a reunion, you may need a negotiator or someone to act for you. Both of you are going to be anxious and emotional.

My adoption manager, Sue, left the job before I could thank her. I could have done with a bit of offloading from all my ups and downs towards the end, but I had my family, and they have been very understanding and supportive throughout. It was sad: I phoned Sue's office to be told she'd had a nervous breakdown, had moved away from the area and had been admitted to a psychiatric ward somewhere. I had known that she'd had personal problems, but I did like her and found her very helpful. I wrote to her office and asked them to pass a card on to her. I needed to thank her and wish her well. I hope she got it.

Today's adoptees will have a total openness with their past, whether it is with the new birth book or through experiencing the new open adoption system, where the adoptees are continually in touch with their biological family. I hope that the parents who have lost their children through hard times pull themselves together, realise their loss, overcome their fears and possibly become reunited with their children in some kind of way. You may never be forgiven, but remember we adoptees are a special breed, a special race – perhaps a new type of forgiveness can be created.

I think it is important to consider all the issues surrounding a search for your birth parents, as this can be a traumatic experience for your adoptive parents and your natural parents. There are a lot of resources readily available on the Internet and from a number of international agencies. There are also many organisations that can help you through the process of becoming acquainted with your birth family or help with issues of rejection. Some of these are charities; some ask for payment. It is worth exploring all the options.

It is going to be an emotionally difficult but hopefully rewarding journey. The first step is the biggest step you'll take. Deciding to begin the journey requires dedication, perseverance and an emotional and mental strength. It may be a quick journey; it may take years. Be prepared for both.

I would say keep your expectations low, your mind open and take one step at a time. Don't get your hopes up too much as it is so easy to get caught up in the moment and leap forward too quickly while emotions are running high.

There is a book out there in the world of adoption, which comes highly recommended. It is called *The Primal Wound: Understanding the Adopted Child* and is by Nancy Verrier. Many people recommend it because they feel it helps explain the feelings and actions of adoptees. I personally found it a very heavy and psychologically intense book. I must admit, I didn't read all of it, but as I scanned it and flicked through the pages I felt more and more like an abnormal, mixed-up, emotionally scarred, psychiatric patient. Maybe I am! Please don't think I am saying this is not a great book – it is; it just wasn't for me. I felt very uncomfortable being put into a category and having every feeling scrutinised, analysed and named. Some sort of theoretical explanation was given for every thought and feeling, for every hang-up and every flicker of insecurity. Perhaps I feel more comfortable being free with my thoughts – and even secretly enjoy being different.

I do feel for the birth mothers and fathers; in a lot of cases, they can never start the search process. The ball is in our court. We adoptees can trace our blood parents, but they can't find us. It was certainly like that in my day.

Adoptees talk a lot about their reunions. I didn't have one, so I really can't comment on it. Yes, I did make contact – or so I believe – but I don't think that can be classed as a reunion. I did prepare for it, though, and was very sad that I was too late.

If you have become inspired by my writing to trace a long lost blood mother or father, what advice could I give you? Every adoptee needs to make sense of their story. Write your own story; it has certainly helped me. An adoption research or reunion journey is a massive step to take. Are you really ready to jump on the boat and head out to sea? It will be a very emotional voyage with lots of choppy water and big waves. The sea is a dangerous place. You will cast your nets and maybe catch nothing. You will have to keep casting your nets and hope for a bite. You're looking for big fish, so you will have to have strong nets and be prepared to keep repairing them. You're going to fall in and get swallowed up, but seawater has healing properties. You're going to have to learn to swim against the tide. Once you're on the island, there is no way back.

Over the last year, I have surrounded myself with the word adoption, and not just in my search. Everything to do with the word has caught my attention, sparked my interest and forced me to become engulfed in the subject. I have sat for hours visiting social network sites. I have spent hours talking to social workers, midwives and adoption professionals. Occasionally, I have felt as if I was drowning in the subject.

It's now time to get on with my life. It has been a rather obsessive journey – interesting and productive – but now I say goodbye to my pain, my questions, my uncertainty and the word adoption itself. I want to move on.

I will always be an advocator of the adoption and fostering systems and will continue to be sensitive to the things I have written about them. There are so many children out there who need a family, guidance, stability and most of all love. Perhaps a better way to look at it is that there are no unwanted children out there, just yet-to-be-found families.

Today is the day I want to stop my journey. I have reached a peaceful island, and I want to stay there. Many people have asked me if writing my story has helped me. My answer to that, if I'm being honest, is no; it has been like going through the whole thing twice – and, if you include a few rewrites, four times. Also, I now know that writing is a very lonely business; it is so different to writing a song. When you write a piece of music, you can share it instantly with others and immediately get input and feedback – listen to this verse, listen to this chorus, have a read of these lyrics, does this melody work with the middle eight? You just can't do that when writing a book; you're on your own with no one to help or give you feedback and advice. Something all us musicians and adoptees need is praise – you just don't get praise sitting by yourself for months and months on end. It's like telling someone a joke and having to wait two years to hear the laughter. Don't get me wrong; I have enjoyed writing this book. In a way, I feel that I have spent my life on my own. I am used to being on my own and have enjoyed my own company over the years. And if I have touched anyone by my writing, then I am very happy.

I have just had an email from Maria, Billie's spiritual friend – the one who told me at the church that Billie may be in contact with me one day. She knew I was writing the final chapter of the book and was keen to pass on some information to me.

Dear Clive,

I had to let you know that late last night I started to get a rush of energy through my body. It was like getting an intense headache of high frequency. This is often what happens when a person who has passed over is trying very hard to come through. The feeling doesn't stop until contact is made. I then had a sense of knowing it was Billie.

I said, "Is that you, Billie?" and I clearly heard her voice saying back to me, "Yes, my dear." We both then laughed, and the intense feeling started to dissipate.

She wanted to convey a message to you. She said what a wonderful boy you are and that she wished she could hold you in her arms like she did when you were a baby. She wants you to know that she is with you and around you at this very special time and so proud of you in all ways.

I asked her if she would be reincarnating and she said, no, she had spiritually ascended now and would be working by guiding others in their work from spirit. I went back into so many memories of her and

our times together sitting in her kitchen. I could see her face so
clearly and hear her laughter and that wicked sense of humour. She is
at peace and her energy is so vibrant and present and part of the
journey of your life, Clive. I had to pass this on to you as she was so
intent to come through last night.

Love Maria x

Thank you, Maria, and please thank Billie.

As I opened the email from Maria this morning I could smell Billie's perfume again. It was a nice message and reassuring to know that Billie is still around. I said to her that I wished I felt more spiritual and had inherited more of Billie's spirituality. She replied, "You have. It lives in your music." Yes, I suppose it does. We jazz musicians just take it for granted. It is good to know I have people around me Billie can use to get in contact with me.

This morning I went round the house and collected up all my notes – my house has been littered with little scraps of paper about things I wanted to say in my book – and burnt them. I have had great pleasure in deleting drafts of my writing from my computer. And all Billie's letters have been put in a big box, sealed with extra-thick masking tape and put in my loft, next to her ashes.

I have gone through the house, found all the hidden empty bottles of whisky and thrown them out – I have just poured the last full bottle down the sink. It helped me get through the massive ups and downs in my search, and now I just don't need it anymore.

Today I'm putting down my pen and finishing my story. I hope you have enjoyed reading it and being on my journey with me. More importantly, I hope my story has helped you understand our world – the adoptee's world – that special and unique world in which all of us live.

I was wanted.
I was chosen.
I was cherished.
I was looked after.
I grew in my parents' hearts.
I was loved.
I was ADOPTED.